THE
HARDER
YOU PREY,
I PRAY!

THE HARDER YOU PREY, I PRAY!

In Jesus's Name
Prayer Book

**A Daily Guide for Encouragement
and Strength for All Families**

**Prayer, Promises and Devotions
for Families And Soldiers**

Joseph Harris

authorHOUSE®

AuthorHouse™
1663 Liberty Drive
Bloomington, IN 47403
www.authorhouse.com
Phone: 1-800-839-8640

Published by AuthorHouse   02/27/2015

ISBN: 978-1-4817-5031-8 (sc)
ISBN: 978-1-4817-5030-1 (e)

Print information available on the last page.

Any people depicted in stock imagery provided by Thinkstock are models, and such images are being used for illustrative purposes only.
Certain stock imagery © Thinkstock.

This book is printed on acid-free paper.

CONTENTS

DEDICATION

This is a book for every soldier of Operation Iraqi Freedom and Operation Enduring Freedom, Afghanistan, our warriors in transition, all soldiers worldwide in conflict and during humanitarian operations, and those who are at home. I pray for every family member. This book is for all soldiers that are United States of America heroes, who have served unselfishly and have given their lives as an ultimate sacrifice for freedom. This book is for those who have stood guard and those who continue to stand watch and guard on all fronts of war for this nation and in support of all people, foreign and domestic, for freedom. They have demonstrated courage, bravery, and heroism beyond expectations.

Soldiers are remarkable citizens and warriors who uphold our democracy and our way of life. I pray God's blessings for all our soldiers in every branch of service, their families, and the United States Armed Forces. May God bless those who stand on every front to protect world freedom and liberty as we know it and expect. Our prayers go out to all families of our fallen comrades. Our prayers go out to every soldier who has survived wars and has injuries as a result. May the Lord be with you and comfort you in every way that only the mighty and loving Lord Jesus Christ can do. I pray that He keeps you in His perfect will. I pray that our Lord Jesus Christ's compassion rests upon every soldier and his or her family. I pray that God watches over all of them and keeps their souls in the palm of His hand. May He grant us peace during the toughest time of war, battles, conflicts, and any measure of extreme violence and terrorism. I pray for peace in every sanctuary and that God would bless us on every battlefield. May the prayers of the church, God's saints, and the power of the Holy Spirit keep us near Him.

What is prey? Prey is anyone or anything that is hunted down with the intent to destroy, devour, or kill. A predator is someone or something that hunts its prey by force. Prey is something that is eaten or consumed by a big animal; a lion in its habitat is the predator. We often see on Discovery channel the lion chasing food to eat. Sheep are prey for a hungry wolf or lion. In church it is similar. Satan preys on people in the church. The people are sheep who belong to God. He places an under-shepherd to preach the gospel, pray, and watch over souls in that church. The scripture declares that the enemy goes about like a roaring lion, seeking whom he may devour. He seeks to devour Christians to destroy relationships and the church. That is why you see so many people falling away from the church.

God wants His people to remain faithful to Jesus Christ until He comes. When they come back, it is because of Jesus Christ. Once they recognize the love of Jesus, they will remain in Jesus. Jesus Christ is our Shepherd, to protect us from being eaten alive. Our prayer lives help us. We must have a constant connection through prayer, speaking to Jesus Christ.

INTRODUCTION

This book consists of prayers that will help everyone throughout the United States military, civilians in all nations throughout the world, and those who desire to have a closer relationship with our Lord Jesus Christ. Please understand that through prayer, everyone who calls on the name of Jesus Christ can receive healing and comfort by His tender love, grace, and mercy. His mercies are renewed every day.

There are many people who experience a relationship with God Almighty during family crisis, conflict, war, famine, natural disasters and many other times. He desires that we seek Him not just during those times of need but at any time in our lives. His arms are always open to catch us and hold us as His personal children. He cares for us. God is always there with you. Leaders and all soldiers desiring a relationship must ask God to enter into their lives. There is no greater joy on earth than to know God and have a relationship with Him. Prayer is communicating with God. Your intimate time with Him is your own special time for a breakthrough by Him. Soldiers desiring our Lord to help in time of desperation will be filled with joy unspeakable. These moments with the Lord will enable soldiers and friends to spend quiet meditations with our Lord and Savior in prayer and supplications.

Prayer changes things in our lives. His word says that the effectual fervent prayer of a righteous man availed much. These prayers are a means of acknowledging our Lord in many ways. This will enable soldiers throughout the world in every branch of military service men, women, and children to remain connected to our Lord. This book will enlighten the hearts of Christian men and women, children of God around the world. These scriptures will allow you to be spiritually inclined in relationship and worship. These daily prayers will help you in your walks with God Almighty. Your life will be more productive than ever before. You ears shall hear God, and He shall hear you.

Your communication with the Lord will never be the same. It will give you a sense of how to defeat the enemy in Jesus Christ when situations arise daily. You will learn to deal with the drama, hurt, sadness, and difficulties that life often deals you. You will learn to have a better relationship with our almighty God in the midst of the enemy's attacks and his desperate attempts to destroy us.

The Lord our God has many ways of helping His children when you have been born again. He helps all who call on Him. He has even proven His love for those who have rejected Him. Nevertheless, we who are followers have to remember that we are in the world but not of the world anymore. Do not be ashamed of the gospel of Jesus Christ. He is not ashamed of you. His dealings are certainly His ways and not man's ways. He said, "Come unto me all who labor and are heavy laden, and I will give you rest. Take my yoke." God tells us in scripture to "cast your cares upon me." God is the God of the living. He sent His only begotten Son that we may have life everlasting. He also sent His Son to give us the abundant life. There are benefits and blessings that enable every one of us to reach our destiny for the glory of God. So whoever you are, do not stop praying. God will deliver you from that situation. In the book of James (5:16), He says, "The effectual fervent prayer of a righteous man availeth much."

ADAPT AND OVERCOME

Then Moses stretched out his hand over the sea; and the Lord caused the sea to go back by a strong east wind all that night, and made the sea into dry land, and the waters were divided. (Exodus 14:21 KJV)

Lord, thank you for using Moses as an example to manifest your power. You used him to set the children of Israel free from Egypt's bondage under Pharaoh's charge.

Lord, you have blessed me in so many situations dealing with bondage. Nevertheless, I still need you to help me adapt and overcome challenges ahead, including those that have risen today. I pray for the kind of faith and power that you gave Moses when he found himself challenged between Pharaoh's army and the Red Sea.

Your word says, **"Moses stretched out his hand over the sea; and the Lord caused the sea to go back by a strong east wind all that night, and made the sea into dry land, and the waters were divided."** It was victory at that moment for the people. He adapted to the wilderness as he led God's people out of bondage through the Red Sea. Father, thank you for helping me adapt to life's challenges in combat and at home.

You have parted so many Red Seas in my life. You made a way out of no way when it appeared that I was trapped in wrong relationships. You helped me overcome the most difficult challenges and struggles that I had to face in this life. When death confronted me with a near miss of a rocket-propelled grenade, you protected me and kept me. When my vehicle was struck by an improvised explosive device, and team members and friends became casualties, you were there to comfort me. You took me through my battlefield experiences. You even kept me through my military career. You kept my enemies at a distance.

I pray that you keep a hedge about my family, friends and fellow soldiers. I pray for those who do not know the power of your deliverance. Much like Moses, Jesus's disciples learned to adapt to circumstances but also overcame many obstacles. They believed in our risen King and Lord Jesus and wrote the word of God under Jesus's authority. Lord, I believe in your word and trust it to be the truth, way, and life that inspires life-changing decisions for all people. Father, be with me as I go about to tell of your goodness and mercy. In Jesus's name, amen.

> *Thus Israel saw the great work which the Lord had done in Egypt; so the people feared the Lord, and believe the Lord and his servant Moses. (Exodus 14:31)*

> **My Faith in God: God knew Moses's faith before he lifted up the staff. Because of his faith and his people, God parted the Red Sea. Have faith in God when the enemy is after you and you don't know what to do. Act on your faith the way Moses did.**

Confess and believe!

Today, I will commit to being adopted by you, Lord Jesus. I believe that you own me and that nothing shall pluck me out of your hands because you are my heavenly Father. You said that you will never leave me nor forsake me.

ADOPTION

*So you have not received a spirit that makes you fearful slaves. Instead, you received God's Spirit when he adopted you as his own children. Now we call him, "Abba, Father."
(Romans 8:15 NLT)*

Abba, Father, thank you that I am no longer a fearful slave in this life to my enemies. Thank you that I am not adopted by the devices of Satan. Nor am I adopted in Spirit by Satan and his demonic forces.

The word *Abba* is an Aramaic word that is known to be closely translated as "Daddy." It was a term that most young children used in addressing their own father. It really conveys a close relationship between a father and his child. It also conveys the trust that a child puts in his daddy. Pray this prayer:

I confess Jesus as Lord of my life. He is my "Daddy" also. I confess that he is my Father. My adoption is by Jesus Christ. I am not adopted nor in the devil's will and possession, because I commit myself to you, Lord Jesus. I pray to be a slave in your will. I pray to be a bond servant to Christ Jesus. I pray your will be done, Lord Jesus, in my life and the life of your people. I believe and receive the adoption as one of your children right at this very moment. I am no longer a tool for the enemy to trample on. I denounce all forms of evil, attacks, and snares of the enemy in my life. I am now at your service, Lord Jesus. I pray to walk under your authority and power. I need your Holy Spirit daily.

I thank you that I can call on your name to rebuke any attacks that attempt to entangle, grip me or place my spirit and soul in bondage. Thank you that I have an inheritance in you. Thank you that you hear me when I cry out for help, Abba Father. You opened your arms as a Father in the beginning to form a relationship, and I accepted you and will always. As your adopted child, you know my circumstances, downfalls, and pitfalls. Whatever it is in life, I know that I can call you, Heavenly Father. Thank you for adopting me during my time of military service and bringing me home safe and sound to my wife and children and entire family. Father, continue to keep me and all soldiers and their families in your adoption, blessings, love, and perfect will.

> **My Faith in God: By faith, I am adopted to my Lord Jesus Christ. He will bless me. There is only one true God that can be found if you seek Him. He is the God of Abraham, Isaac, and Jacob. He is the one who sits on the throne in heaven. False gods will try to challenge and hinder you.**

Confess and believe!

Today, I have received the Spirit of God who made me whole. I will commit to being adopted by you, Lord Jesus. I believe that you own me and that nothing shall pluck me out of your hands because you are my heavenly Father. You said that you will never leave me nor forsake me.

AFFLICTION

For our light affliction, which is but for a moment, is working for us a far more exceeding and eternal weight of glory. (2 Corinthians 4:17)

Lord, I am thankful that you know all things and allow certain things to happen in my life to get my attention. However, I ask for faith and patience through my afflictions. I know my outcome will be because of my faith in you and your decision.

Help me as you helped your servant Job through his pain and suffering in his body. You helped him through the loss of his family. Help me through my family situations. Encourage us through our trials. Job's wife told him to curse God and die, but Job persevered through his affliction and demonic obstacle. Lord, you allowed him to endure because of your comfort and love. Job said, I know that my redeemer lives and in the latter times, he shall appear even though my body fades away. Lord, I will trust you at all times.

Lord, lift me up where I am broken, and place me in your presence with the kind of faith you gave Job during his suffering. Job did not lose faith because you gave him strength to make it through the difficulties he faced. Father, give me the kind of faith to persevere through afflictions. I pray for those blessings that will come from your glory. You name is glorified forever. In Jesus's name, amen.

My Faith in God: My faith takes me to the riches of God. I am not concentrating on afflictions. I am concentrating on healing.

Confess and believe!

My current afflictions and old wounds cannot stand against the power of God in my life. I will not allow any wounds to keep me from the blessings that remain laid up in heaven and on earth for me. Blessed be the name of the Lord, who took away my afflictions and filled my heart with His spirit of joy and peace. I will keep my mind on Him who sits on the throne in heaven and who sends healing to the needy.

ANCHOR OF MY LIFE

This hope we have as an anchor of the soul, both sure and steadfast, and which enters the Presence behind the veil, where the forerunner has entered for us, even Jesus, having become High Priest forever according to the order of Melchizedek. (Hebrews 6:19-20)

Lord, thank you for anchoring my soul. I submit myself to you today. Thank you for guiding me during my combat deployments. You gave me hope in the nick of time. You constantly watched over me and helped me through multiple missions. You even gave me a mind to trust you in all things. My trust is indeed in you, Father, because you keep my heart, my mind, my soul, and my life in your hand. I am confident that I am anchored in you.

I will be steadfast in my walk with you Lord. I pledged it when I became born again in the front of the church after my pastor preached the sermon on the lame man in Acts 3. My entire future eternally and on this earth is secured in you, Lord. With you on my mind, I can conquer all things through the strength you give. You give the perfect solutions to life. You gave your only Son for life to be sustained. You are the anchor of my soul, spirit, and mind. Lord, you are my strength. I pray that the Holy Spirit keep me anchored each and every day. Lord, I am grateful that you have given me life at this very moment. I pray for continuous obedience and humility. I pray to evade and escape my enemy and the disobedience that arises in my life. Lord, I ask that you keep my spirit and strength in your perfect will.

My Faith in God: Jesus Christ is my High Priest. He is over all things through the Father. He is the anchor of my soul.

Confess and believe!

Today, I confess my agreement with my wife and my friends that whatever you have for me and my family and friends we shall receive. I confess and believe in your supernatural power.

ANCHOR ME, LORD!

This hope we have as an anchor of the soul, both sure and steadfast, and which enters the Presence behind the veil, where the forerunner has entered for us, even Jesus, having become High Priest forever according to the order of Melchizedek. (Hebrews 6:19-20)

Lord, keep my speech plain, and as I help others in need. I praise you for anchoring me in your love and compassion that never fails. When life gets heavy, I pray that you continue to come to my rescue to lift loads of burdens off me. Help me through complications, confusion, and turmoil. You see the best in your servants and those who call on your name. I pray your transforming power on family, friends, and those I serve with, including my chain of command. I pray for your anchoring power in their lives. Anchor them to make decisions by consulting you first. Anchor their families to the love of Christ Jesus. Whatever they are asking for, help them believe and walk in expectation of your blessed power. Lord, I pray to be anchored in your word and faith and live with you forever. All glory and honor to the name Jesus Christ, Son of the living God.

My Faith in God: I walk in faith to know Him and that I will be in His presence to receive blessings.

Confess and believe!

Today I will commit to being anchored every day to you, Lord. Use me for your glory. Jesus, I believe that you own me and that nothing shall pluck me out of your hands because you are my heavenly Father. You said that you will never leave me nor forsake me.

ANGER

So then, my beloved brethren, let every man be swift to hear, slow to speak, slow to wrath; for the wrath of man does not produce the righteousness of God. (James 1:19-20)

Lord, you know my conditions better than anyone, including myself. I pray that you help me to get rid of my anger issues so I may be in the righteousness of God. Change my ways to be more calm, compassionate, affectionate, and loving in your sight to others. Keep my tongue that I may speak according to your word with edification. Help me to speak kindly to others at all times.

King David said to you in his moment of hurt and self-exposed sin of adultery, "Create in me a clean heart, O God; and renew a right spirit within me." When I am deployed to war in a distant land, and the danger of combat is all around me, keep me in your perfect will. Guide me by your Holy Spirit so that wrath will not build up in my heart. Guide me to walk under your righteousness daily. Keep me as your child through these battles of life.

My Faith in God: Faith helps me also to hold my tongue so I will not speak out of order. When I speak, believe by faith that goodness will spring forth.

Confess and believe!

I will commit to hearing you, Lord, and my loved ones and friends. I pray also to be slow to speak, avoid wrath and anger situations, and walk in the peace and joy of the Lord. I confess and believe to be the righteousness of God.

BUILD AN ALTAR

Then Noah built an altar to the Lord, and took of every clean animal and of every clean bird, and offered burnt offerings on the altar. And the Lord smelled a soothing aroma. Then the Lord said in His heart, "I will never again curse the ground for man's sake, although the imagination of man's heart is evil from his youth; nor will I again destroy every living thing as I have done." (Genesis 8:20-21)

Father, thank you for accepting Noah's offerings on the altar to worship and glorify you. Thank you for showing us the importance of altars and sacrifices. We demonstrate obedience and a heart to please you. We acknowledge that we hear your voice.

Noah, Abraham, and other men of God built altars to honor you, demonstrating their personal relationship and your goodness. They realized that you dwell at altars because they symbolize holiness. So when your Spirit is present, we can experience a renewing, awakening, and blessings that flow in abundance.

You made it possible for us to come before you at any time. Thank you that I am allowed to come as living sacrifice, holy and acceptable in your sight, Lord. I pray that you purge me and wash me whiter than snow. Create in me a clean heart, and renew a right spirit in me, at the altar or anywhere you choose to bless me. I pray to be acceptable in your sight. Lord, I lay every weight at the altar today. I surrender to you in complete submission. Transform me into a man of God who will follow you, under the influence of your Holy Spirit, in Jesus's name, amen.

My Faith in God: My faith encourages me to build an altar in God's honor so that I can send prayers to you, Lord.

Confess and believe!

Today, I confess to building something in this lifetime to please God.

AGREE

Again I say unto you, That if two of you shall agree on earth as touching any thing that they shall ask, it shall be done for them of my Father which is in heaven. (Matthew 18:19 KJV)

Father, you know my loved ones, my friends, and those who need prayer for whatever reason. Help me touch in agreement with them all in a spirit of agreement. Help me come into agreement with my battle buddies while we are deployed to this foreign land. You said if two of us agree on earth as touching anything, it shall be done. We touch in agreement as we face our toughest moments, in combat deployed and combat at home. Help us through struggles and hardships. Help us be in agreement as teams, units, and organizations and as leaders and subordinates.

Lord, we pray that you shape our lives through this experience to be pleasing in your sight. Keep us in your heart, Lord, and send your Holy Spirit to keep us, and help us glorify you even when we do not understand things. In Jesus's name, amen.

> **My Faith in God: If two of us agree, faith can move many things into and out of our lives. Faith in Jesus pleases God.**

Confess and believe!

Today, I confess my agreement with my wife and my friends that whatever you have for me and my family and friends, we shall receive. I confess and believe in your supernatural power.

ANGELS

The angel of the Lord encampeth round about them that fear Him, and delivereth them. (Psalm 34:7 KJV)

Lord, thank you for your angels that you created for your purpose. Lord, send your angels to encamp around me and my brothers and sisters while I am in this warring country, overseas or in any designated place the military has sent me. I pray that your angels are with my unit while we face daily missions. Protect us, and deliver us home safely to our loved ones. Lord, we thank you for all that you have done. In your precious name, amen.

My Faith in God: Your faith brings angels to encamp around you. God wants to fulfill your destiny. Faith makes things happen because God is pleased with your faith.

Confess and believe!

Today, wait on God to send angels to encamp around you. They will be in your presence even when you not aware of them or expecting them.

ANXIETY

*For the strength of the wicked will be shattered, but the Lord
takes care of the godly. (Psalm 37:17 NLT)*

Father, you are the God who can take away anxiety and fear. Keep me
in your perfect hand of healing. Keep me calm by your Spirit. Because
anxiety is fear that tries to destroy your people, I bind it by the power
of the Holy Spirit. I pray for the Holy Spirit to destroy it and remove all
thoughts associated with it. I pray the anointing power of God to remove
all strongholds with negative spirits chasing my life in an effort to destroy
me. Lord, remove any anxieties by your grace and mercy.

I am thankful for all you do. I believe in Christ Jesus with all my heart and
that I can do all things through Him. So I believe that this prayer will break
through barriers of my heart and all of me. Since I believe in you, Lord,
help me to walk in peace as I rebuke fear. Strengthen your servants on the
battlefield in Iraq and Afghanistan to stand against fear and the enemy
abroad. Strengthen us to stand against any trouble at any given time. You
made me a soldier, so I count on you to be with me regardless of any
situation or outcome. You already know the beginning and the ending.

Your power is mighty in protection and care. Your power helps us see
things in reality. Your power is mighty and unlimited in blessings. You
even said in the second epistle to Timothy that you did not give us the
spirit of fear but of power and love and a sound mind. I pray for all my
brothers and sisters in Christ. I pray for those who have not tasted of His
goodness in sound conscience in hopes that they partake in your love and
increase in the power of faith. In Jesus's name, amen.

**My Faith in God: My faith is to know that God will
take care of me in any and all situations.**

Confess and believe!

Today, I will commit to the Lord's strength over my life. His strength
sustains my life.

APPLE OF HIS EYE

Keep me as the apple of your eye; hide me under the shadow of your wings, from the wicked that oppress me, from my deadly enemies who surround me. (Psalm 17:8-9)

Father, keep me as the apple of your eye. Thank you for looking at me with love just because you love me, just because you are the God of love. There is no other like you. Help me to experience and recognize your loving kindness while I am deployed in this terrible war. Help me experience and know your blessings even when the enemy comes near my house and attacks. Help me know the sign of attack that I may call on your righteous name in time of need.

If you would be so kind, Father, place a hedge about me home as you see fit. Help me see your blessed power through my enemies and storms while deployed to Iraq or Afghanistan. Nothing is too hard for you. When David called on you in his heated battles, you were there. When Gideon called on you in his battles, you were there. When Joseph called after being betrayed by his brothers, you were there. In all cases, you blessed them even more with your saving grace because you recognized them as the apple of your eye. Blessing and honor to your name, Lord.

My Faith in God: I believe that He keeps me as the apple of His eye.

Confess and believe!

Today, I submit to God to hide me in the palm of His hand. Keep me near Jesus Christ. Keep your angels in my life for protection.

THE ARMOR OF GOD

Finally, my brethren, be strong in the Lord and in the power of his might. Put on the whole armor of God, that you may be able to stand against the wiles of the devil. (Ephesians 6:10-11)

Father, thank you for knowing that I need strength in my life. I need strength because of the demons that prey on me in the attempt to destroy my life and the ministry set forth for me. You are the strength of my life, and I praise you for protecting me right now. You are the one who makes me new when I am broken. You know how to make me strong when it seems the enemy has my life.

Finally I am able to experience the power of your love. I see creation clearer. I could not see before, but now I can see. Finally, I am stronger because of your Holy Spirit in my life. Finally, I can see a glimpse of your might. I saw you turn my enemies away. Now that I am on my second deployment, my prayer is that you turn evil away again. Dress me in your armor, Lord, that I may stand my ground against the wickedness and evil that tries to take my life—and my family's as well. Lord, I need every part of the armor you provide. In Jesus's name, amen.

My Faith in God: My faith is to be strong in Jesus Christ. I will not think that I am weak. I will only thing and know that I am one of God's Soldiers.

Confess and believe!

Today, I confess to wear the armor of God for protection against every dart that the enemy throws, regardless of what it may be. God's power is more than enough.

BAPTISM

Know ye not, that so many of us as were baptized into Jesus Christ were baptized into his death? Therefore we are buried with him by baptism into death; that like as Christ was raised up from the dead by the glory of the Father, even so we also should walk in newness of life. (Roman 6:3-4 KJV)

Lord, help me make a decision today to get baptized according to Matthew 28. I desire to become a new creature in Christ Jesus. Because I have accepted Jesus, the enemy sees me as easy prey. I know my God sees all the predators that wish to keep me out of God's will.

I pray for newness of life before my baptism and after. Lord, thank you for your Holy Spirit guiding me to be obedient in getting baptized. Father, I thank you that through your Holy Spirit working in my new life, I can now witness effectively to others I know and those I meet. I praise you for helping me in obedience to your command and affirming my relationship with Jesus. I thank you that today I can walk in newness of life because I believe in you, and your word says I can walk in the newness of life. Keep my faith strong in you, Lord. In Jesus's name, amen.

Heavenly Father, my next goal is to immediately get baptized after accepting Jesus as my personal Savior. You set the example with your Son, Jesus, when He was baptized in the Jordan River by John the Baptist. Father, you said, "This is my beloved Son, in whom I am well pleased" (KJV) Matthew 3:17. Lord, you said we were buried with Him through baptism into death, that just as Christ was raised from the dead by the glory of the Father, even so we also should walk in newness of life. Lead me in the spirit to walk and not waver in the things of life but look to Christ in my new walk and please you, Lord.

My Faith in God: I will believe His holy word and confess that He died and rose from the grave to save me from God's wrath. Now, I believe that my prayers count against all predators. The Lord has purposed for me to live with Him forever.

Confess and believe!

Today, I confess that Jesus rose from the dead for sinners to accept Him. His love extends beyond the grave and death. Exalt His name.

OVERCOME BATTLES

All those gathered here will know that it is not by sword or spear that the Lord saves; for the battle is the Lord's, and he will give all of you into our hands. (1 Samuel 17:47 NIV)

Father, your servant David said, "The battle is the Lord's." Lord, increase my faith to know that there is no battle too great for you. Give me the power like you gave David to prevail over the Philistines in my life.

Goliath was a predator, but David was a poor shepherd boy who knew God. My giants are many things that appear to be dominant to overtake by fear and power. But I will not live with fear and doubt. Give me the confidence to know that you will take care of all my enemies.

Help me this day in battle even in Iraq and Afghanistan. Strengthen me through this mission just as you did in the past. Strengthen my fellow soldiers all around me. Lead me through the different missions and patrol routes. Lead me through the hot weather conditions and the heat of the battle that I may confront. Lead me through the hot spots of battles I face daily. You know the twisted environments we deal with. You know the trying times and the frustration of trying to capture the enemy. Help me be strategic and disciplined during my time deployed.

Help me this day to be stronger and wiser. Allow the power of your words to be my protection. Bless me to use your word as David used one stone to slay the enemy that came against God's people. Then turn the hearts of my enemy so that they will praise you, O sovereign Lord. All praise to your holy and righteous name.

My Faith in God: My faith is to know that all power is in His hand. I believe no weapon formed against me will prosper.

Confess and believe!

Today, I confess that all my battles belong to the Lord. He will fight for me. He will sustain His people, regardless what the situation appears to be. What it looks like does not count because my God is all-sufficient.

OVERCOME BITTERNESS

Pursue peace with all people, and holiness, without which no one will see the Lord: looking carefully lest anyone fall short of the grace of God; lest any root of bitterness springing up cause trouble, and by this many become defiled; lest there be any fornicator or profane person like Esau, who for one morsel of food sold his birthright. (Hebrews 12:14-16)

Lord, help me as I endure this time on the battlefield where my heart might grow weary and become bitter. I pray for peace. Only your love and kindness can remove the root of bitterness that tries to take its place in my heart. I pray to pursue peace with all people, regardless of my situation. I can only imagine and experience this peace in your grace and mercy. You are the only way to true holiness.

Grant me a portion of holiness even in this country where I am fighting. I pray your blessings upon my unit and all their leaders this day. I pray even for my enemies all around and about me. It is only your love and peace that enables me to surrender to you and to pray for all men and all people.

Keep us in perfect peace in the midst of Iraq, Afghanistan, and even at home in the United States of America. You hold the key to all peace that surpasses understanding. So anxiety has no place because of your love. In Jesus's name, amen.

> **My Faith in God: My faith allows me to seek peace with all men and to be an overcomer in all things. We are to fellowship with one another. This will please God because the Love of God is shed abroad to help us overcome our present condition.**

Confess and believe!

Today, I confess that God has removed any bitterness and that I now walk in peace. God gave it to me, and no one can take it away.

TIMES IN TOUGH BATTLES

I returned and saw under the sun that the race is not to the swift, nor the battle to the strong, nor bread to the wise, nor riches to men of understanding, nor favor to men of skill; but time and chance happen to them all. (Ecclesiastes 9:11)

Lord, help me when I have battles and confusion about them. Only your wisdom can take me through the days and nights when I experience battles. You know the times when they approach and try to take over my heart. Keep me through the time of despair. Keep me through unforeseen attacks only you see. Help me know that I am always on your mind as I experience troubles on every side of my life. In the midst of combat you already know my pains. In the midst of my marriage, you knew the day and time when the battle would start. You even know the limits of my battle and troubles. You control time and chance; therefore my trust is in you. Be with me during the times and chances that await me. I understand that at any time something could happen to change the course of my life. I understand that the plans you have in my life remain even during the battles in my life and through the deployments to Iraq and Afghanistan. You hold the key to all things of life and to my life. Create in me a heart to know you better. In Jesus's name, amen.

My Faith in God: My faith is in the Lord Jesus who holds time and chance in the palm of His hand.

Confess and believe!

Today, I confess that God holds the future of my life and that He knows all things under the sun and blesses according to His will for us.

VALIANT SPIRIT IN BATTLE

And what more shall I say? For the time would fail me to tell of Gideon and Barak and Samson and Jephthah, also of David and Samuel and the prophets: who through faith subdued kingdoms, worked righteousness, obtained promises, stopped the mouths of lions, quenched the violence of fire, escaped the edge of the sword, out of weakness were made strong, became valiant in battle, turned to flight the armies of the aliens. (Hebrews 11:32-34)

Lord, thank you for a valiant spirit in battle. You always know how to come through to give your servant victory even in the sight of defeat. No predator can take my as prey because I am in your hands. You gave me a strong foundation of faith that keeps me in the right mind here in Iraq and Afghanistan. You give me the mind to be valiant even at home, where it seems that the enemy is still chasing me. But the enemy has a problem. It is because my strength is in you, O sovereign and righteous Lord. The problem to the enemy is that the harder they prey, the harder I pray.

Nothing by any means overtakes me from you, Lord. You are my strength and my salvation. You are my rock and my protector. You are my strong tower. You are my Lord. It is your power that guides me and builds my confidence and faith all the day and night and each moment of the day. I will praise you every day, Lord, for what you have done in my life and for things yet to come. I will hold to your promises as did David, Samuel, and the prophets. Blessed be your holy and righteous name. In Jesus's name, amen.

My Faith in God: My faith is also built in God because He reveals His past warriors of faith who please Him.

Confess and believe!

Today, I confess that Jesus is my Lord. Our Father made Him King of kings, Lord of lords. I am encouraged by my Lord and those heroes of faith that God appointed for set time in the Bible.

BELIEVE

And Thomas answered and said to him, "My Lord and my God." (John 20:28)

Father, thank you for revealing yourself to me much as you did to Thomas. When I was not sure that you had risen from the dead, you proved it to me. Because you have been so gracious is revealing your loving kindness, I now believe you and your healing power. Thank you for comfort in my heart and in areas that may have been damaged. You know how to heal just right. Lord. Much like Thomas, I acknowledge you because my eyes have seen enough to know that you are real. Thomas could testify that you had risen in the glory of the Father in heaven. You always reveal truth through our eyes as we see your creation and lives sustained under the power of the blood of the lamb. You allow us to touch and feel the evidence of your creation. Your made known your presence in the twinkling of an eye. Father, I pray that others in the armed forces and other places around the world will be convinced through your touch and through stages of life with you on my side. I believe that you died and rose with all power in you, Lord. Help those that have unbelief. In Jesus's name.

My Faith in God: My faith is to be strong in Jesus Christ. I will not think that I am weak. I will only think and know that I am one of God's soldiers.

Confess and believe!

Today, I confess my agreement with my wife and my friends that whatever you have for me and my family and friends, we shall receive. I confess and believe in your supernatural power.

BRIDGE THE GAP

And behold, there was a great earthquake; for an angel of the Lord descended from heaven, and came and rolled back the stone from the door, and sat on it. (Matthew 28:2)

Building bridges is a specialty of many construction firms. It was also an occupation I took up in the military. Bridges have many classifications, and they can be extremely heavy. We built many bridges with precision, discipline, and motivation. We always completed them for support of field commanders and their soldiers who desperately needed a way in and out of the heat of the battle or who needed them for simple support missions. In old World War II footage, you can see the importance of having a bridge in combat. In many cases it determined the success or failure of large military organizations and field commanders. The purpose was always to win the war.

Father, thank you for your love than never runs out. When I was so far away, lost and confused, you bridge the gap for me to come back to God. You even stretched your hands out time and time again. You always make me feel loved. Thank you Lord for being their even when I was so distant. Your love is the best because it comforts me. e

Lord, thank you for the act of atonement bridging the gap so I can approach our Father in heaven. Lord, help me bridge the gap with friends and all people by showing the love of Jesus Christ. Help me be a bridge specialist, bridging the gap by witnessing to other soldiers in war. You have demonstrated that no gap is too wide, and no bridge is too far. Thank you that there will never be another gap between us. In the name of the Lord, amen.

> **My Faith in God: You give us the choice to go across the bridge that was built perfectly for us. Jesus died to build the bridge for all of us to the Father.**

Confess and believe!

Today, I confess that Jesus has already bridged the gap for my life. I can come to God now and every day for the rest of my life.

BROKEN AND USED

Now to each one the manifestation of the Spirit is given for the common good. To one there is given through the Spirit a message of wisdom, to another a message of knowledge by means of the same Spirit, to another faith by the same Spirit, to another gifts of healing by that one Spirit, to another miraculous powers, to another prophecy, to another distinguishing between spirits, to another speaking in different kinds of tongues, and to still another the interpretation of tongues. All these are the work of one and the same Spirit, and he distributes them to each one, just as he determines. (1 Corinthians 12:7-11 NIV)

Heavenly Father, you used your precious Son, Jesus, to carry his cross to Calvary; he died on the cross to redeem me from my wretched way. He rose in the tomb with all power for me. He left the tomb to show Himself alive. This represented the most important demonstration of Jesus love. Jesus died and destroyed sin's power. He blessed me; He blessed mankind.

Lord, thank you because you left us gifts to do a good work on this earth to witness and represent you. You remind us that all the gifts are of the same Spirit. You reminds of the power in those gifts in that they get results. Father, increase my confidence and faith so that I will use my gift to glorify your name. Help me to walk in faith and recognize my purpose in life. With you Lord I can do all things through Jesus Christ because of the strength he gives me on the inside.

My Faith in God: Faith in Jesus Christ helps me rely on the gifts of the Spirit which will bring me out of my brokenness to be used by God. No more pity parties, instead I will walk by faith in the Spirit.

Confess and believe!

Today, I confess my desire is to be used by God to bring Him glory.

BURDENS LIFTED

> *Then Joseph could not restrain himself before all those who stood by him, and he cried out, "Make everyone go out from me!" So no one stood with him while Joseph made himself known to his brothers. And he wept aloud, and the Egyptians and the house of Pharaoh heard it.*
>
> *Then Joseph said to his brothers, "I am Joseph; does my father still live?" But his brothers could not answer him, for they were dismayed in his presence. And Joseph said to his brothers, "Please come near to me." So they came near. Then he said: "I am Joseph your brother, whom you sold into Egypt. But now, do not therefore be grieved or angry with yourselves because you sold me here; for God sent me before you to preserve life. For these two years the famine has been in the land, and there are still five years in which there will be neither plowing nor harvesting. And God sent me before you to preserve a posterity for you in the earth, and to save your lives by a great deliverance." (Genesis 45:1-7)*

Lord only you know my burdens and the extent of those burdens within my heart. You know the beginning to the end of my life, not to mention the how I feel when trouble comes my way. Only you can stop those storm of life. Your power is always the solution over the enemy.

Joseph's brothers were burdened with the illusion that Joseph was dead because of their decision to put him in a pit and leave him to die. Joseph was burdened because he knew that his father thought that he was dead, and he was unable to contact him. As Joseph revealed himself to his brothers, they were instantly astonished and amazed, and burdens were lifted from each brother. The war and the battle within were over. Joseph's burden was lifted as well to know that his father, Jacob, still lived.

Burdens are a strange type of suffering but can also strengthen and help us make right choices the next time. This is an example of how God uses brothers to express brotherly love during the time of burdens or difficult conditions. This is also a story of a young man who rose to power after displaying godly discipline and love to the enemy and his brothers while in bad conditions.

Soldiers experience burdens of war where they have to adjust and adapt to environments daily while under pressure. Today God wants you to know that whatever burdens you during your deployment, He is able to deliver you. Put your mind at rest. He wants you to trust Him above all things that exist. He is your Father and the keeper of your soul.

Lord, help me have an attitude like Joseph's, who was thrown in a pit but came out of the situation as the second in command of Egypt. Bless my brothers at home and here. Restore any situation that harmed my relationship with my family. Remove all burdens, because I need you and I believe in you. I praise your holy name, Lord Jesus.

> **My Faith in God: There is only one true God, who can be found if you seek Him. He is our all-powerful and sovereign God.**

Confess and believe!

Today, I confess my agreement with my Lord Jesus Christ that He has lifted my burdens and delivered me from my old life.

A SOLDIER'S
SECOND CHANCE

Now there was also a dispute among them, as to which of them should be considered the greatest. And He said to them, "The kings of the Gentiles exercise lordship over them, and those who exercise authority over them are called 'benefactors.' But not so among you; on the contrary, he who is greatest among you, let him be as the younger, and he who governs as he who serves. For who is greater, he who sits at the table, or he who serves? Is it not he who sits at the table? Yet I am among you as the One who serves.

"But you are those who have continued with Me in My trials. And I bestow upon you a kingdom, just as My Father bestowed one upon me, ³⁰ that you may eat and drink at My table in My kingdom, and sit on thrones judging the twelve tribes of Israel." (Luke 22:24-30)

Lord, thank you for giving me another chance. You are the one who loves like no other. You are the one who knows the heart and searches me for my well-being.

My Faith in God: I have faith in my second chance for life. I will start a new life today by faith in Jesus Christ, no matter what is going on in my life. I will not put Jesus on hold any longer. Forgive me, Lord Jesus.

Confess and believe!

Today, I confess my agreement with my Lord Jesus Christ with thanksgiving and praise that I will honor Him during my second chance in life.

CHILDREN, OBEY YOUR PARENTS

Children, obey your parents in the Lord, for this is right. "Honor your father and mother," which is the first commandment with promise: "that it may be well with you and you may live long on the earth." (Ephesians 6:1-3)

The Lord commands children to honor and obey their parents. Obeying your parents gives God glory and honor.

Lord God, help me and my wife connect with children everywhere. Help us train children up, so that they will not depart from the faith. Thank you for instilling through your ministry the importance of obeying God and parents. Help me teach my children, even while I am deployed, to fight battles in their lives. Help my children listen to your voice, that they may become obedient in your will and purpose. Thank you, Lord, for helping us follow what is right in your sight. Keep us under your authority to follow your commandment.

> **My Faith in God: I have faith in God that He will strengthen me to follow His command. I will honor and obey my parents. I will walk by faith in Jesus Christ.**

Confess and believe!

Today, I confess my agreement with Jesus Christ to obey my parents according to the word of God. I will obey Jesus's command to honor my father and mother.

COMBINED FORCES

But you shall receive power when the Holy Spirit has come upon you; and you shall be witnesses to me in Jerusalem, and in all Judea and Samaria, and to the end of the earth. (Acts 1:8)

Heavenly Father, only you can unite forces to win campaigns that lead to freedom and democracy. Only you can bring peace to a violent world. We desire peace over all wars, in your precious name, Lord. At home, Lord, we need our military forces to unite with supreme power to overcome the enemy. I pray for peace and that the president, vice-president, secretary of defense, secretary of state, supporting Cabinet members, and people who make a change and impact may reach a resolution that will deter war and conflict to bring about peace.

However, if coalitions have to war, unite all branches of service to formulate a strategy through prayer to bless policies and agreements that will enable peace and resolve this war and those all around us. Father, I pray that you send your angels to guard against outbreaks that fuel fires in war. Encamp your angels around all leaders and combined forces that their decision making, character, ethics, and morals will be advantaged to bring about peace.

Lord, you are righteousness alone. Help us do the right thing in every situation. I am thankful, Lord, that you have set aside legions of angels to protect us, serving you according to your will and purpose. I still believe that when two or more of your people come together in agreement, you are present, and you answer prayers. Help our nation, and help me, Lord, to be that leader to participate in fighting the war with other services that will support us. Help me to be safe daily in my daily operational missions throughout the world.

You illuminate the importance of combined forces. Father, we depend on you to help combined forces of good over combined forces of evil hearts. We acknowledge your sovereign will and hope for humanity to live in peace. In Jesus's name, amen.

My Faith in God: I have faith in your combined forces. I believe that all the saints will come together on your behalf at your calling only. My faith is that we will receive the power as you planned for us, Lord.

Confess and believe!

Today, I confess my agreement with my Lord Jesus Christ that He has control of all combined forces throughout the world and will use them for His glory. Use me, Lord Jesus, in your combined forces.

THE POWER OF CONFESSION

Whosoever therefore shall confess me before men, him will I confess also before my Father which is in heaven. But whosoever shall deny me before men, him will I also deny before my Father which is in heaven. (Matthew 10:32-33 KJV)

Lord, empower me to confess of your goodness to all people that I come across. Help me during my deployments to tell of your grace and mercy. I pray to speak and testify of how you blessed me while serving in the armed forces and even when I retired from service. All praise to your righteous name.

I confess that I need you right now in my time of weakness and when it seems like there's no end to war or no end to troubles in my life. I confess that I will always need you even in the battlefield of life. Jesus, I confess that you are the Son of God, and I believe that you rose from the dead with all power by your Father in heaven. You gave me life, and thank you. In Jesus's name, amen.

My Faith in God: I have faith in the power of confession. I confess by faith that Jesus is in my heart and He guides me daily. I confess that His power has changed me, and my life is better, for the glory of God.

Confess and believe!

Today, I confess before all of humanity that Jesus Christ is my Lord and Savior. He redeemed me by His blood. He made me a new creature in Jesus Christ.

CONFIDENCE

Cast not away therefore your confidence, which hath great recompense of reward. (Hebrews 10:35 KJV)

Father, thank you for encouraging me to keep my confidence. You strengthened me to have more courage and faith. Lord, in my weakest moments in life and while I served in the armed forces, you lifted me up when I felt low and lacked confidence. Help me be strong and confident in my job performance on the battlefield and during all my unit missions. Help me to have confidence in my family. Help my marriage survive this deployment time and when I come home. Lord, I ask you to help me put all my confidence in you for the rest of my life.

My Faith in God: I have faith and confidence in Jesus Christ for my life, no matter how life deals me a blow. I have confidence that Jesus will always see me through and reward me according to His will and pleasure.

Confess and believe!

Today, I confess to be in agreement with my Lord Jesus Christ that I will walk in confidence because of His word, His will, and His way.

COURAGE

Have I not commanded you? Be strong and of good courage; do not be afraid, nor be dismayed: for the Lord your God is with you wherever you go. (Joshua 1:9)

Lord, as we continue our missions in foreign countries such as Iraq and Afghanistan and all other deployments, we ask you to strengthen and encourage every soldier through every difficult moment, every mission that we are called to complete. Help us to be strong and courageous when the time comes to engage enemy forces.

We pray for peace. But God, you know all things. So help us to be the force you planned us to be. Help us to be strong and courageous even in our thoughts.

We are reminded that you will never leave us or forsake us. Give us the necessary encouragement we need, Lord, to survive on the battlefield. Give us courage as we engage hostile forces. Give us courage with our families. Build us up when the family is in distress because of our absence from home. In the blessed name of Jesus Christ our Lord, amen

> **My Faith in God: Lord, you gave me faith to have courage. I pray for courage to overcome my trials and battles. My faith keeps me from being discouraged because the power of God is in my spirit and my life. He will never leave me or forsake me.**

Confess and believe!

Today, I come into agreement with you, Lord, to be strong and courageous like Joshua, in Jesus's name.

CRUCIFIXION

And He, bearing His cross, went out to a place called the place of a skull, which is called in Hebrew, Golgotha, where they crucified Him, and two others with Him, one on either side, and Jesus in the center. (John 19:17-18)

Lord, thank you for sending your Son, Jesus Christ, to die for my sins. Men have been tortured in many ways to pay a price for kings and princes and royal leaders around the world. But not one of them sacrificed himself for humanity and realized results except Jesus Christ, the Son of God. Some men have been beheaded, hanged, or shot by firing squads. So many people have been executed for many reasons. But there has never been one to pay the price like our Lord Jesus Christ, nor did they become a living sacrifice. Jesus carried His cross to the death ground, Golgotha, to pay a penalty for mankind.

Lord, I thank you that you took on the sin of the world in your body and destroyed it, that I might have life in the abundance. You made eternal life available by your love. Lord, help me to crucify my flesh that I might submit to your will and become a follower of your army, in your grace and love and kindness. You alone died for me because of your unlimited and amazing love. In Jesus's name, amen.

My Faith in God: I believe that Jesus died and rose from the dead for my sin. Therefore I will praise and serve Him.

Confess and believe!

Today, I come into agreement with you, Lord, that you already finished redeeming your people. You defeated the enemy, death, and the grave. There is no one like you. All glory to your righteous name.

DESTINY

But rise and stand on your feet; for I have appeared to you
for this purpose, to make you a minister and a witness both
of the things which you have seen and of the things which I
will yet reveal to you. (Acts 26:16)

Lord, thank you for controlling my life's destination. You are the revealer of all things, because power is in your hands. You are mighty and powerful beyond comprehension and imagination. You take us beyond life's blessings and expectations with your goodness. You are the center of my life because you are my strength and you know me. You know my mind and body and my soul and where I will end up. I believe in heaven when the time comes. You hold time and the future destination in your hand. You have predestined us for your purpose. You know what my life has in store before I know it. You appeared to me to make me a minister of your gospel.

Lord, I pray that my destiny is for the uplifting of your kingdom. I pray to give you all the glory in all things. Lord, while I am here in Iraq, help me understand even more that I have a destiny to love other people. I have a destiny to live a good life beyond measure. I have a destiny to be victorious in battle under your mighty hand of protection and obedience. I have a destiny to lead and follow in various situations of life. I have a destiny to be the priest of my house. I have a destiny to be successful in life. I have a destiny to learn your word and walk in it. I have a destiny to have the mind of God.

In destiny, you chose me. Lord, help me recognize these areas of my life so I will be submissive to your will to stay on the path of righteousness. Lift me up from the crooked places, that I may know your power. You know if I will end up in heaven or hell. You know if I love life and your way. When things are out of control and dysfunctional at home and even in battle, remind me to be strengthened in your love and kindness. You know all things in heaven and earth. Create in me, as King David said, a clean heart. Renew a right spirit within me.

My Faith in God: I believe that the Lord has a destination for me on this planet as well the time to go.

Confess and believe!

Today, I come into agreement with you, Lord, that you already finished redeeming your people. You defeated the enemy, death, and the grave. There is no one like you. All glory to your righteous name.

DESERTED

And those who know your name will put their trust in you; for you, Lord have not forsaken those who seek you. (Psalm 9:10)

Lord, thank you for the many times you have not forsaken me. I praise you because you have not deserted me. You could have left me because of my ways in this body at times. Help me to keep on seeking you. During my stay here in Iraq or Afghanistan, help me in time of trouble. I know now that you are the God who sees me through all my problems, pain, and agony, even my struggles. Your power to keep me is so wonderful that it is difficult to contain my joy in the lord. Worthy is the Lamb. In Jesus's name.

My Faith in God: My faith is in you, Lord, because you have never deserted me. Every time I need you, I can count on you.

Confess and believe!

Today, I put my trust in you for everything, whether good or bad. I trust you with my life and possessions. My lips will forever praise you. There is no one like you. All glory to your righteous name.

Dwelling in
the Secret Place

He who dwells in the secret place of the Most High shall abide under the shadow of the Almighty. I will say of the Lord, "He is my refuge and my fortress; my God, in Him I will trust." (Psalm 91:1-2)

Father, I thank you that you have a secret place for me to dwell. You understand all people and everything about us. You know the complications of war. You even understand those who have not found their secret place. You understand the complications of separation between family and friends.

Lord, I pray that, just as you protected David when he went up against his enemies, you will protect me and my friends and my fellow soldiers in battle against my enemies. Protect my fellow soldiers against their enemies as they deploy to do battle in foreign lands. Help me and my team as we carry out the mission to protect our liberties and help others in time of need. I pray to abide under your protection for all things, for you are almighty and all-powerful. I also pray to continually be in your secret place in the spirit of the Lord. And because of this, I give you praise forever, my Lord and my Redeemer. In Jesus's name, amen.

> **My Faith in God: My faith is in you, Lord, because you have never forsaken me. Every time I need you, I can count on you. In my secret place, you are there to advise me.**

Confess and believe!

Today, I put my trust in you for everything, whether good or bad. I trust you with my life and possessions. Lord, Take over all my secrets, so that I will be free. My lips will forever praise you. All glory to your righteous name.

WAIT ON JESUS

Wait on the Lord; be of good courage, and He shall strengthen your heart; wait, I say, on the Lord! (Psalm 27:14)

Lord, thank you for giving me patience to wait and faith to believe in you. You have moved in my life. Father, help me continue to wait on you even when I face troubles in my way. Help me have courage and a strong heart to know that you will always be there for me. I thank you for removing the troubles and fear that attacked me. Trouble won't last always because you always show up and pull me out of situations I find myself in. Even while I am deployed for combat in Iraq or Afghanistan or any hostile country, fighting for peace, you always keep me protected in your perfect will. All glory and honor to your name.

I now know that you are my light and my salvation and that I do not have to fear. I believe in your word that no weapon formed against me shall prosper. I believe that I can cast my cares on you because you care. Trouble can never have the victory as long as I know that you are my God, the one who rose from the dead, the one I worship, praise, and glorify. Lord, continue to strengthen my heart and my mind where you see my weaknesses. I know that all people fall short. But it is your love and kindness that changes my heart. I believe from this day on that my troubles are defeated, in Jesus's name. I will walk in victory regardless, because you have ordained it.

My Faith in God: My faith is in you, Lord, because you have never left me helpless. Every time I felt week, you strengthened me.

Confess and believe!

Today, I am determined to wait on God's move in my life. Whether it is today or tomorrow, I will walk in courage and in God's strength. All glory to your righteous name.

EXALT HIM

Therefore God also has highly exalted Him and given Him the name which is above every name, that at the name of Jesus every knee should bow, of those in heaven, and of those on earth, and of those under the earth, and that every tongue should confess that Jesus Christ is Lord, to the glory of God the Father. (Philippians 2:9-11)

Lord, your Son, Jesus, is highly exalted. I pray that my life may exalt Jesus Christ, who redeemed me. You changed the course of my life. You are worthy to be exalted forever. You gave the world a second chance at life here and everlasting life. I magnify you, Lord, and worship your name. I honor and bow before you. I rejoice in your name. I lift up my hands to the name of Jesus in full worship. My heart and voice sing praise to thy name. Holy, holy, holy is thy name in all the earth, heaven, and creation. I pray by the power of the Holy Spirit that all your people and everyone in this world and the angels may exalt your precious name, Jesus. In Jesus's name I pray, amen.

My Faith in God: It is my faith in you, Lord Jesus, and what you have done for me that allows me to bow down and worship you. I confess that you are my Lord, and I glorify you.

Confess and believe!

Today, I am in agreement with the Holy Spirit to exalt your name. I pray for all soldiers to read and know this scripture. In fact, all families of the earth must read and know this scripture. Jesus's name is above all names.

FAITH

Now faith is the substance of things hoped for, the evidence of things not seen. (Hebrews 11:1)

Heavenly Father, give me faith in the things I hope for and have not seen with my eyes. Help me have faith in you, Lord, because you are the foundation of faith. Whenever trouble and difficulty arise in my life, remind me to have faith that you will take care of me, no matter what. As I go out to serve the armed forces, give me a great faith that things will turn out as you desire them. Increase my faith to know that I can count on your forever presence and your hand on my life. Increase my faith so that I can always know you will take care of my family. But more important, strengthen my faith in you, Lord, daily. In the holy name of Jesus, amen.

My Faith in God: My faith in you, Lord, brings about manifestation. The things you promise come into existence. I am confident because you called the world into existence and framed it by your words. I will use my faith today, expecting my life to turn around. I will trust you, Lord.

Confess and believe!

Today, I confess that my faith works because God recognizes my faith in Him. My faith must be activated if I want results from God. He will move on my behalf because of genuine faith in Him.

MY FATHER IN HEAVEN

I speak what I have seen with My Father, and you do what you have seen with your father. (John 8:38)

Lord, thank you for being my Father. In you I believe, and in heaven and eternity. I pray to keep honoring you as my Father because you are God. I thank you that you supply my need as a father does. I thank you that you help me grow as a father. I thank you that you help me with my identity of knowing the power of your love and grace.

Keep me in your perfect ways while in Iraq, Afghanistan, or anyplace that the armed forces have sent me. Help me to never turn away to any false gods or images that portray a father identify. Protect me from the evil one who lurks to persuade that he is a father. He is the father of lies and hate and evil. But God is the father of grace and mercy and compassion. Therefore I will trust in you with all my heart and lean not to my own understanding and acknowledge you in all my ways Proverbs 3:5-6.

> **My Faith in God: My faith is in my Father in heaven. He knows exactly what to do for my life. Place your faith in God.**

Confess and believe!

Today, I confess with my tongue that Jesus is Lord. I speak it because of what He has done in my life and because He is who God made Him. I have seen results in my life. Do you remember when He saved your life from death and the grave, when you were on the highway, in a fight, or in some situation when you needed Him?

SERVE GOD, NOTHING ELSE

*No one can serve two masters; for either he will hate the
one and love the other, or else he will be loyal to the one
and despise the other. You cannot serve God and mammon.
(Matthew 6:24)*

Father, I acknowledge you as my only Lord and Master. You have been my
master for all my life. Walk with me, and protect me from the wiles of the
enemy. Keep the darts from trying to poison my mind with false and fake
beliefs. Please be my Lord and Master, for the enemy tries to make himself
my god. Lord, help me confirm my obedience and loyalty to you and you
alone. Help me to put no other before you.

Lord, help me with my finances. Let them not be the center of my life.
Let money not rule my heart or any part of my life. I exalt you and you
alone,

Father. I rebuke all the evil devices and manipulations of so-called gods
and masters trying to take your place. I give you all the honor, praise,
worship, and glory. I pray blessing, honor, and glory to your name forever
and ever. I will put all my trust in you only and serve you wholeheartedly
throughout eternity. Lord, it is you alone that I call Master and believe
with all my heart to be my Lord and Savior. God is Master any way you
look at it. No one is righteous, supreme, and sovereign but you, Lord. In
Jesus's name, amen.

**My Faith in God: Faith helps me serve God and nothing
else. My faith ties me to God over everything else.**

Confess and believe!

Today, I confess that Jesus is my Master and that I will serve Him and not
that person in flesh form.

FULFILLMENT

> *"The Spirit of the Lord is upon Me, because He has anointed Me to preach the gospel to the poor; He has sent Me to heal the brokenhearted, to proclaim liberty to the captives and recovery of sight to the blind, to set at liberty those who are oppressed; 'o proclaim the acceptable year of the Lord."*
> *(Luke 4:18-19)*

Lord, because you are the fulfillment of God's plan of salvation, I thank you. Because you are the fulfillment of our healing and peace and joy unspeakable, I thank you. Thank you that you have the anointing power and authority to preach the gospel to me and all your people, poor in spirit and brokenhearted. Thank you for your blessings that give us sight to see again.

Thank you, Lord, that while I am in the battle in a strange land, I can trust in your power to accomplish things in a perfect way. I can also trust in your power to lead and guide me. My prayer is that you will staty with me through my storms and quiet them with your perfect power of peace. Repair the damage in my heart, and comfort me in my brokenness according to you perfect will of fulfillment. Then Lord, place the Spirit of the Lord upon me that I will be pleasing in your sight for service as a witness to the light of the world. In Jesus's name, amen.

My Faith in God: Faith helps me walk in my purpose of what Jesus has for me.

Confess and believe!

Today, I believe in the power of God and that Jesus came and fulfilled the plan of God. Nothing has gone undone by God the Father. It is time for you to confess Jesus as Lord. Ask Him to show you your purpose.

I AM THE LORD

I am the Lord your God, who brought you out of the land of Egypt, out of the house of bondage. (Exodus 20:2)

Father, thank you for delivering me out of bondage. You delivered me for your purpose. Thank you for abundant life today. You delivered us from bondage in Egypt. You broke the enemy's attack from full oppression of me and my family. I am so grateful to you, Lord God.

No one but you has the power to bring me out of circumstance as such. There is no one like you! Your love is so gentle and perfect. You love me and give me good things. You are the one who blesses my very being. It is because of you I exist. Life without you would be total darkness and bondage. You always mean the best for me. You brought me out of darkness in my life, that house of bondage. You brought me out of debt and brokenness, that Egypt. You brought me out of messed-up relationships. You allow me to walk with you to learn your ways. Thank you for giving us the law through Moses and also ensuring that the law is not what set us free. You gave us Jesus to set us free. He did exactly that when he carried the cross, was crucified and buried, and rose from the grave. In your first commandment of the ten, you said we shall have no other god before you. In the second commandment you said we shall not make for ourselves a carved image.

Lord, guide my life that I may not sin against you. Through your power help my mind to remain on you as the only supreme God of heaven and earth, the creator of all things. I acknowledge you as my God, Redeemer, and Savior. In Jesus's name, amen.

My Faith in God: Faith helps me to come out of any house of bondage. What bondage are you in today? Activate your faith in the Lord Jesus Christ, and He will bring you out.

Confess and believe!

Today I align myself with God, believing that He is the Lord our God. I confess to you, Lord, that I do not have any other God besides you.

HEALING POWER

Likewise the Spirit also helps in our weaknesses. For we do not know what we should pray for as we ought, but the Spirit Himself makes intercession for us with groanings which cannot be uttered. Now He who searches the hearts knows what the mind of the Spirit is, because He makes intercession for the saints according to the will of God. (Romans 8:26-27)

Heavenly Father, I am standing in the authority of Christ Jesus for healing and deliverance for my loved ones and all my friends. In the blessed name of Jesus, I bind all infirmities and strongholds of sickness that attack their bodies and minds and hearts. I pray that you loose your healing power into their situations. Thank you that you are the healer of our lives.

Thank you for the Holy Spirit, who makes intercession and requests to God on our behalf according to His purpose and will for our lives. You have all the answers and all the plans for my life. Keep me in your perfect ways.

Keep my family as I depart to war. Show them the saving grace that you have shown me. Help my children know that you can heal, and you can save anyone from any situation. I pray healing for now and even when I depart this place of war. Keep my mind fixed on you and your power, that I may exalt you forever. In Jesus's name, amen.

My Faith in God: Faith helps me to call on God in prayer to intervene in my life. When my tongue does not say it all, my faith speaks louder to the living God. He already knows me, but I still acknowledge Him.

Confess and believe!

Today, I confess that I will communicate with Jesus Christ, my healer. I walk in by faith that I am healed in those areas that I claim by Jesus's authority. Lord, let your will be done.

HOPE

***Now faith is the substance of things hoped for, the evidence
of things not seen. (Hebrews 11:1)***

Father, help me never lose hope. I believe in you. Nothing is too hard for
you, Lord. I will keep my hope because of your inspiration of life. I want
to be one who has hope engraved in my heart and know that you can do
all things.

I read in your word that "I can do all things through Christ Jesus." It does
not matter what the family situation, God is working behind the scenes
and on the scene, working in many cases directly before us. A mother who
gave birth never gave up on hope. Moses's mother had hope to give up her
son, Moses, in the Nile river and later worked in the palace to raise her
son. That is hope.

Solomon in his wisdom had two women brought before him, with a baby
that belonged to one of them. His decision was to divide the baby between
the two women. The real mother gave up the baby for love. I believe both
she and Solomon had hope that the situation would work out as it did.
The baby went to the actual mother.

God is a God of hope, and He never leaves or forsakes us.

> **My Faith in God: I will walk in hope because of my
> faith in God. What is the one thing you hope for? God
> knows the level of my hope and can change things. He
> controls the outcome of life. Nevertheless, you have a
> choice today.**

Confess and believe!

Today, I confess that my hope is in Jesus Christ, who is my solid Rock.

REMAIN HUMBLE

Therefore submit to God. Resist the devil and he will flee from you. Draw near to God and He will draw near to you. Cleanse your hands, you sinners; and purify your hearts, you double-minded. Lament and mourn and weep! Let your laughter be turned to mourning and your joy to gloom. Humble yourselves in the sight of the Lord, and He will lift you up. (James 4:7-10)

Father, your word tells me to remain humble. You used the prophet Samuel to speak to King Saul of this matter. You told him, "When you were small in your own eyes, were you not heading of the tribes of Israel? And did not the Lord anoint you king over Israel?"

The Lord wants us to obey Him and be humble in His service. Keep the Lord on your side. One of the best ways to knowthat God is on your side is to remain humble and obedient before Him. Saul did not, and he lost the kingdom and his anointing. The Lord wants you to remain loyal to Him. He wants to bless you. God loves those who are humble at heart.

James 4:10 says, "Humble yourselves in the sight of the Lord, and He will lift you up." What a magnificent promise. God knows about your deployment and your return home before you take either one. He desires to keep you in the palm of His hand. But you may need a relationship with Him. If you do not know Jesus as personal Savior, then you need to visit a local church of born-again and baptized believers.

My Faith in God: My faith in God keeps me humble before God. Lord, strengthen me to surrender myself to you each and every day.

Confess and believe!

Today I confess that my God will always be there for me, to help me and make the enemy flee if he attacks me. I will also speak that Jesus is Lord to the glory of His Father in heaven.

NEVER HOPELESS AGAIN

If a man die, shall he live again? All the days of my appointed time will I wait, till my change come. (Job 14:14 KJV)

Father, thank you for upholding me when the enemy attacked my body and mind, much like your servant Job. I thought for a while that I would die, but you helped me maintain my faith even when it was severely tested. You sustained my life, my identity, the love in my heart, and who I am today.

I am more than convinced this day that you are and always will be my Lord and Redeemer. All the days of my appointed time will I worship and wait for your return. Meanwhile, I will exalt you as you keep me in your love and compassion.

My Faith in God: My faith in Jesus Christ will cause me to live and reign in Him forever.

Confess and believe!

Today, I confess that I will live with Jesus Christ all of my appointed time. I will wait for Him to return.

MARRIAGE

What therefore God hath joined together, let no man put asunder. (Mark 10:9 KJV)

Lord, you said that a man and woman who are married should remain together as one and let nothing come between them. Father, I thank you that your word stands alone and never changes. You signified this first marriage with the first family, Adam and Eve. You made her his helpmate.

Regardless of the distance that deployment may cause for my family, keep us strong. Lord, strengthen the vows in my marriage as I go off to war in a foreign country. Allow my wife to know that my heart is with God and with her. Help me during this deployment. Show me how to express my love to her before I depart. It is my prayer to you, Lord, that I be strong in every way, especially my marriage, because my spouse means so much to me. Keep my spouse safe, and allow our hearts to grow fonder of each other in love.

My Faith In God: When it comes to my marriage I will pray hard and consistent against all prey.

Confess and believe!

Today, I will commit to being adopted by you, Lord Jesus. I believe that you own me and that nothing shall pluck me out of your hands because you are my heavenly Father. You said that you will never leave me or forsake me.

SWIFT TO HEAR

So then, my beloved brethren, let every man be swift to hear, slow to speak, slow to wrath; for the wrath of man does not produce the righteousness of God. (James 1:19-20)

Yes, Lord, I will listen to your instructions and obey you. Your word tells me to listen. I believe now that my ears have been closed from your voice. Because you have blessed me, I now know that I must praise your name while I give you thanks. Now I know that I must learn to listen to you. Lord, help me by the power of your Holy Spirit to listen intently and hear your instruction to me. I depend on you from now on to listen to my wife, my children, and all those around me. Lord, I need your help to listen to my family. Lord, I will listen to you, no matter what.

I know you were with me during that mission. I know you saved me for your purpose. I owe my life to you Lord Jesus. I now know that you can do anything.

> **My Faith in God: When it comes to listening to others and closing my mouth to really understand, I will pray for righteousness.**

Confess and believe!

Today, I confess that I will open my ears and listen to you, Lord, by faith.

GETTING THROUGH PAIN

Now the Lord said to Samuel, "You have mourned long enough for Saul." (1 Samuel 16:1 NLT)

Getting through pains, whether present or past, is a blessing because God intervenes and requires others to as well. It could be an addiction or any kind of suffering, yet the Holy Spirit gets us through it.

Father, thank you for helping me in getting through past pains. You told Samuel that he had mourned enough. Help me when I seem to want to keep mourning over past guilt or circumstances. Thank you for reminding me that you are Almighty God, and all the power in comforting comes from you. Lord, allow me to see what you saw in David, the future king, and not look back on the old king, Saul. Help me to have an attitude of moving on to the future and not desiring those in the past to have any effect in my life. I pray that there is no more doubt and heaviness of the past keeping me pent down from my blessings . . .

My Faith in God: I will listen to the voice of God just like Noah and your great prophets.

Confess and believe!

Today, I confess that I will open my ears and listen to you, Lord, by faith.

56

Blessings Given in Return

But he that knew not, and did commit things worthy of stripes, shall be beaten with few stripes. For unto whomsoever much is given, of him shall be much required: and to whom men have committed much, of him they will ask the more. (Luke 12:48 KJV)

Father, my prayer is that you lead me by the hand in your great work. I pray by faith to please you. Since you have given me so many things, I praise you. However, I need your Holy Spirit to lead me under your power. Since you have an assignment for me even while I am here in Iraq, I ask to hold your hand as I serve you. I praise you and ask that you bless me any way you desire. In Jesus's name, amen

> **My Faith in God: My faith will help me carry out the Christian service you placed me in. Whatever my role is as a Christian, help me walk in your Holy Spirit so I can fulfill your requirements.**

Confess and believe!

Today, I confess that you have given me much. I will serve you based on your word, Lord Jesus. Nevertheless, I need your Holy Spirit to guide me.

PRAISE HIM ANYWAY

I will extol thee, my God, O king; and I will bless thy name for ever and ever. Every day will I bless thee; and I will praise thy name for ever and ever. Great is the Lord, and greatly to be praised; and his greatness is unsearchable. (Psalm 145:1-3 KJV)

Lord, you are greatly to be praised because your greatness and your goodness have no measure. You are without limits. My heart cries out to you, Lord, that you will keep me in your hand of salvation and your strength so that I may be pleasing in your sight.

The Lord helps me when I feel discouraged. Praise Him when times are rough. Praise Him in the middle of the night. Praise Him when things seem impossible. You see, He makes possible what seems impossible. He can turn anything around. That's God all by Himself. No wonder the psalmist said, "I will extol thee, my God, O king; and I will bless thy name forever." No one can make the sun shine but Him. No one can make the stars shine but Him. No one can make the moon appear but Him. He deserves all the praise forever. In Jesus's name.

> **My Faith in God: With my faith, I acknowledge the greatness of God as my God and the one and only true and wise God. There is no one like Him. He is the God of my life.**

Confess and believe!

Today, I lift up your name with praise. I will praise you forever because of who you are. I will tell the world of your greatness.

IN THE MIDNIGHT HOUR

And at midnight Paul and Silas prayed, and sang praises unto God: and the prisoners heard them. And suddenly there was a great earthquake, so that the foundations of the prison were shaken: and immediately all the doors were opened, and every one's bands were loosed. (Acts 16:25-26)

Father, help me by your Spirit while I am in Iraq and when I get home to keep praise and prayer on my lips. Help me glorify you in my combat situations. When the day comes and when the midnight hour comes, help me make it through those nights. When I have been mistreated and hurt by others, let that midnight pain go away as I keep my lips praising you.

When I praise your name, I believe that doors will be opened, and my attitude will reflect that I have been set free from captivity and the enemy's immediate attacks. I thank you, Lord, for a refreshing feeling of joy. I believe that there will be a supernatural experience by your presence intervening in my life. When the doors are opened, I believe that my troubles will be cast down according to your word.

In John 15:7, you said that if I abide in you and your word abides in me, I can ask whatever I wish, and you will grant it. When my praise and prayer connect with your perfect word and will, I believe that you will hear me wherever I am, even in Iraq and Afghanistan. Lord, I believe you will hear my lips praising you, regardless of where I am or my state of mind, because you are sovereign and omnipotent. You are the God who inhabits our praise and the same God who is in heaven on your throne. You are everywhere and all-powerful. Lord, help me to keep a committed attitude of prayer, praise, and worship each day. In Jesus's name, amen.

My Faith in God: It is my faith that tells me you will be there for me when no one else can imagine my thoughts, pain, and urgency for help. By faith sing your favorite song. Sing it, and watch the Holy Spirit help you. Magnify Him during your worst moments in life. Your faith in prayer and praise brings deliverance. Break every chain and shackle in your midnight hour. It is not over until God says it's over. Exalt Him in the midst of the enemy. War zones will not be able to stop you. His love will take over your life.

Confess and believe!

Today I believe that if I sing praise to you, Lord, with all my heart, chains of darkness, sin, and rebellion and the clutches of Satan will no longer grip me. You have all power, and your mercy gives me strength.

BLESS THE CHILDREN

Despise not one of these little ones; for I say unto you, That in heaven their angels do always behold the face of my Father which is in heaven (Matthew 18:10 KJV)

Father, you know all things. Nothing under the sun can hide from you. You know my family inside out. You know my children. Lord, you even know my children's sadness and happy moments. You know the pain of the disease my child bore. I thank you because you control all things. When my child told me that in her dream, she saw the hand of God healing her, she saw the holy angels curing her mind, and she saw His hand as he touched her. The next morning she had been cured of the last report of cancer. I thank you, Father, that even while I am in Iraq, you reign from everlasting to everlasting. In Jesus's name.

My Faith in God: With my faith, I acknowledge that God looks out for the little ones and has angels watching over them.

Confess and believe!

Today, I believe that Jesus's angels are guarding little ones and telling Jesus everything about them.

LEADERSHIP

For it was fitting for Him, for whom are all things and by whom are all things, in bringing many sons to glory, to make the captain of their salvation perfect through suffering. (Hebrews 2:10)

Heavenly Father, we come before you with thanksgiving. Thank you for keeping all of us safe and strong during this time of war. Today, we ask for your blessings as we assemble here for such a special occasion of inducting some of the army's newest noncommissioned officers into the NCO Corp, better known as "the backbone of the army." Lord, be with them as they represent this great army with the highest of professionalism. Help them in their responsibility to live up to the NCO creed. Grant them the Warrior Ethos Spirit of victory and never defeat. Remind them of the importance of duty, honor, country, and most of all God first. Grant them the attitude of being strong and courageous.

Now we ask that you watch over and protect them as they seek to perform their duties. Your word says you shall give your angels charge. Lord, we thank you for watching over us this day and in days to come. Father, we also ask that you grant the safety of our families, friends, and loved ones. Bless them as they wait patiently during the remainder of this deployment for their loved ones to return. In the name of our Lord and Savior, Jesus Christ, amen

My Faith in God: With my faith, I acknowledge my salvation and your protection. Keep your mercy on me.

Confess and believe!

Today, I lift up my hands with praise because of your wonders in leading people even when we do not deserve your leadership and care. Thank you for your grace.

PUT ON THE WHOLE ARMOR OF GOD

Finally, my brethren, be strong in the Lord and in the power of His might. Put on the whole armor of God, that you may be able to stand against the wiles of the devil. For we do not wrestle against flesh and blood, but against principalities, against powers, against the rulers of the darkness of this age, against spiritual hosts of wickedness in the heavenly places. Therefore take up the whole armor of God, that you may be able to withstand in the evil day, and having done all, to stand. (Ephesians 6:10-13)

Father, I stand on your word because it is the power of salvation. Your word is the armor that is needed to stand. In my life I am in the armed forces. I am a soldier who needs your care above all. I ask you, Lord, that you help me be equipped with your armor. Place each piece of your armor on me to hold me up while I do battle with my enemy, whether it is carnal or spiritual. Lord, protect all of me in your armor. Protect my heart, my mind, and my spirit man. Help me study your holy word to strengthen and encourage me as well. Thank you, Lord, for the helmet of salvation and the sword of the Spirit. Thank you for all pieces.

My Faith in God: With my faith, I acknowledge that my armor is greater than the enemy's attacks.

Confess and believe!

Today, I believe in the power of Jesus Christ and how He protects from my enemies. I completely trust in God.

THE LORD'S PRAYER

Our Father which art in heaven, hallowed be thy name. Thy kingdom come, thy will be done in earth, as it is in heaven. Give us this day our daily bread. And forgive us of our debts, as we forgive our debtors. And lead us not into temptation, but deliver us from evil: for thine is the kingdom, and the power, and the glory, forever. Amen. (Matthew 6:9-13 KJV)

Father, help me set an example in modeling prayer as Jesus prayed. Lord, I believe you know my every need before I ask it of you. Thank you for being my daily bread, for filling my need and preparing for others. Thank you for the power to forgive. Father, help me forgive my fellow soldiers regardless of what I am going through. I thank you, Lord, that you have the power to grant such blessings. You have the kingdom and all the power and glory in your hand. I thank you that you are able to deliver me from temptations and from getting on the wrong course of life. My prayer is to stay in your kingdom, that I might serve you, walk with you, and talk with you each day of my life, even while on the battlefield. In the precious name of Jesus, amen.

My Faith in God: With my faith, I believe the power of God can move mountains out of my way. He moves mountains in combat and at home.

Confess and believe!

Today, I believe in the power of Jesus Christ moving mountains that try to hold me back from worshipping and serving God. I am an overcomer in Jesus Christ.

COMMUNION

For I have received of the Lord that which also I delivered unto you, that the Lord Jesus the same night in which he was betrayed took bread: and when he had given thanks, he brake it, and said, Take, eat: this is my body, which is broken for you: this do in remembrance of me. (1 Corinthians 11:23-24 KJV)

Heavenly Father, I confess my sin before you and submit my life to you that I may recognize the importance of communion. You said to do this in remembrance of you. I thank you for your body being broken for me. I thank you for your shed blood on Calvary that destroyed sin and washed me whiter than snow. The power of your blood destroyed all manner of sin in its totality, disease, sickness, and brokenness in my life. As I accept Jesus Christ as my personnel Savior and declare my devotion and commitment to my Lord, now I partake of the communion, that which honors and celebrates my Jesus Christ, my Lord, as we expect His great return. Rejoice in our Lord Jesus Christ, and exalt His name forever. Lord, my desire is always to commune with you forever. Celebrate with the Lord and His people.

My Faith in God: With my faith, I acknowledge partaking in the celebration called communion to celebrate Jesus Christ as the One who died and rose from the dead.

Confess and believe!

Today, I lift up your name, Lord Jesus, with praise. I confess and humbly thank you, Lord, for allowing me to partake in the Lord's communion.

FAMILY

> *Now Adam knew Eve his wife, and she conceived and bore Cain, and said, "I have acquired a man from the Lord." Then she bore again, this time his brother Abel. Now Abel was a keeper of sheep, but Cain was a tiller of the ground. And in the process of time it came to pass that Cain brought an offering of the fruit of the ground to the Lord. Abel also brought of the firstborn of his flock and of their fat. And the Lord respected Abel and his offering, but He did not respect Cain and his offering. And Cain was very angry, and his countenance fell. (Genesis 4:1-5 KJV)*

Father, help me take care of my family. Help me seek you for sound advice at all times. You gave Adam the first family and instructed him to be fruitful and multiply. You gave him a wife. He did as you said. Lord, you conveyed to me that my spouse and children are to be obedient and honorable in your sight. You also gave Adam a family so he would not be alone and so he could express his love to someone who was apart and special to him. Help me, Lord, to be the head of my house and connected to my family, teaching them your ways of righteousness, your commandments, and a proper lifestyle in obedience and loving kindness. Help me connect my family with military programs that are family enriched as well. Help me always express my love, protection, concern, and commitment to my family, friends, and fellow soldiers.

My Faith in God: With my faith, I will acknowledge that God requires obedience, and I will be obedient to God from this point on in my life.

Confess and believe!

Today, I lift up your name with praise. I ask you, Lord, to strengthen my family.

HUSBAND, LOVE YOUR WIFE

Nevertheless let every one of you in particular so love his wife even as himself; and the wife see that she reverence her husband. (Ephesians 5:33 KJV)

Heavenly Father, thank you for my marriage with the one I love so dearly. Even during the rough and rocky times in my marriage, I am grateful. I am grateful because you continue to bless me regardless of my failures and mistakes.

I am reminded that you said, "Therefore what God has joined together let no man separate." This assures me that you *designed* marriage, making it acceptable in your sight. You said to love her as I love myself. Help me live a covenant marriage with the one I love. Help me understand my commitment and sacrifice to you as well as my loved one. Help me have a strong, intimate relationship with her. Help me love my wife as Christ loves the church. Lord, keep me encouraged through the good times and the hard times. Even when I fall short of my commitment in my marriage, you manage to lift my head above water. So, Lord, strengthen my marriage where it is weak. In the name of our Lord, amen.

My Faith in God: With my faith, I will love God and my spouse

Confess and believe!

Today, I confess that Jesus always comes through regarding my relationship.

KEEP YOUR MARRIAGE STRONG

For this cause shall a man leave his father and mother, and shall be joined unto his wife, and they two shall be one flesh. (Ephesians 5:31 KJV)

Father, my wife and I made a vow to love each other till death do us part. We pray to keep our marriage strong. We pray to not even discuss the word *divorce*. We will not give the enemy a reason to exploit.

Guide me in conforming to my wedding vows and the holiness and sanctity of my commitment to my spouse. Help me renew my vows daily in my mind and heart with my loved one—not just when trouble arises, but daily in the spirit of the Lord.

You gave the standard for getting divorced. And you always allowed love to rule over the enemy's attacks. Jesus said that Moses established the law of divorce because of the hardness of man's heart. But Lord, you also said, two shall become one flesh—no longer two, but one flesh. Therefore what God has joined together let no man separate. You even said that if they divorce each other, they commit adultery the one against the other

Thank you, Lord, for allowing me to know the meaning of divorce and marriage. Lord, help me not to get a divorce. Guard our marriage against outsiders and the enemy. In Jesus's name, amen.

My Faith in God: With my faith, I will obey God to love my wife as Christ loves the church.

Confess and believe!

Today, I confess that it was Jesus who fixed my marriage and helped me to become a better person.

FINANCES

"Bring all the tithes into the storehouse, that there may be food in My house, and try Me now in this," says the Lord of hosts, "if I will not open for you the windows of heaven and pour out for you such blessing that there will not be room enough to receive it." (Malachi 3:10)

Lord, I know everything I have is because of you. I know that the first fruits of my goods belong to you, no questions asked. You said to bring all our tithes to the storehouse that there might be meat in your house. Help me manage my finances. Help me create a budget that will keep me out of debt. Lord, help me in obedience in all aspects of my finances. Guide me into obedience in paying my tithes, offerings, and bills, that I may please you with a cheerful heart. I desire to honor and bless you, Lord. You said to prove you, that you will pour out of the windows of heaven and give blessing so vast that I will not have room to receive it all. Lord, help me become a better steward with the money you give me. Lord, help me each time I must give tithes and offerings. In Jesus's name, amen.

My Faith in God: With my faith, I acknowledge God as the one who helps me to manage my finances.

Confess and believe!

Today I thank you for blessing me with finances. You control all finances and the economy.

MY BODY IS A TEMPLE

Know ye not that you are the temple of God, and that the Spirit of God dwelleth in you? If any man defile the temple of God, him shall God destroy; for the temple of God is holy, which temple ye are. (1 Corinthians 3:16-17 KJV)

Lord, help me treat my body as your temple. You said you dwell inside my body. Help me control my sinful urges. Help me to fast that I might feel your presence even more.

My body is for your purpose. Lord, keep me from the abusive ways of cigarettes, alcohol, and drug addiction and any other substance abuse. Help me overcome my drug or alcohol addiction. Help me that these addictions will not destroy me. Be forever present, O Lord of my temple. Father, help me be obedient in controlling my flesh. Lord, help me avoid abuse of my body so I can serve you in your kingdom.

My Faith in God: With my faith, I acknowledge to God that my body is a temple to reflect His work inside me.

Confess and believe!

Today, Father, you know all things in the body and the temple. Complete in me a clean heart.

GET SPIRITUALLY FIT

Therefore we also, since we are surrounded by so great a cloud of witnesses, let us lay aside every weight, and the sin which so easily ensnares us, and let us run with endurance the race that is set before us. (Hebrews 12:1)

Lord, you said to run the race and fight the good fight. You also said to press for the prize of the high calling of God. Father, help me improve the level of fitness in my life. In my spiritual life, Lord, I pray for fellowship and study of your holy word. Help me understand what you are saying to me on a daily basis in my Spirit-filled life. Keep me fit to do battle against the enemy. Even when I deploy, Lord, help me call down prayer before I go on multiple missions.

My Faith in God: With my faith, I acknowledge that God has changed me to become some who walks in the Spirit

Confess and believe!

Today, I lift up your name with praise. I will praise you forever because you alone blessed me and removed the weights from my life today.

HUMILITY

Let this mind be in you which was also in Christ Jesus: who, being in the form of God, thought it not robbery to be equal with God: but made himself of no reputation, and took upon him the form of servant, and was made in the likeness of men: and being found in fashion as a man, he humbled himself, and became obedient unto death, even the death of the cross. (Philippians 2:5-8 KJV)

Help me have a humble spirit and a mind like yours, Lord. Help me in my daily job, my military occupational specialty. Also allow me to be a servant with the Spirit in me. Help me crucify my selfishness that I may be more humble. Help me serve others by laying aside my self-serving desires. Be with me as I serve the military during this crucial moment in history. Help me get rid of my selfishness and pride by helping others. Lord, I desire to be humble before you and others. You never tried taking over or being God, but you allowed the Father to use you for His plan of salvation. You said, "Humble yourself under the mighty hand of God, and that He mayhe will lift you up." In the name of Jesus Christ, Lord and Savior, amen.

My Faith in God: I will use my faith to walk in the mind of Christ as I live this life and face all challenges.

Confess and believe!

Today, I confess a new mind and humility in my life by the power of the Holy Spirit. Thank you, Lord Jesus, and I magnify your name!

CHRISTIAN

God has not given us a spirit of fear, but of power and of love and of a sound mind. (2 Timothy 1:7)

Lord, help me be an effective Christian to walk in your anointing. Remove fear and doubt. In my dealing with real people, strengthen me and encourage me in the Spirit and through prayer.

Lord, I pray for a bold spirit that will not agree with fear. I pray to stand against enenmy attacks. You gave your disciples a mind like yours to do your work and will for your kingdom. I pray for you on the battlefield and before I deploy. Lord, you said I can do all things through Christ who strengthens me.

My Faith in God: I will use my faith to express the power, love, and disciplined mind of Christ, whatever I am going through.

Confess and believe!

Today, I rebuke all my fears and confess God's power over my life in every way!

CONTENTMENT

Let your conversation be without covetousness; and be content with such things as ye have: for he hath said, I will never leave thee, nor forsake thee. (Hebrews 13:5 KJV)

Lord, help me make you the priority of my life, not material things. Help me give to others. Thank you for the abundance that you have already given me through my military job, my civilian job, and many other blessings. Allow me to be content and not desiring what I do not need. Help me be a blessing to others.

My Faith in God: I will use my faith to be content that Jesus Christ will always be with me.

Confess and believe!

Today, I am satisfied in Jesus Christ because He holds my life in His hand! Lord, I exalt your name!

BLESSED

Blessed is every one that feareth the Lord; that walketh in his ways. For thou shalt eat the labour of thine hands: happy shalt thou be, and it shall be well with thee. (Psalm 128:1-2 KJV)

Lord, thank you that you I can walk in your ways. Help me keep walking in your ways as the head of my house. I pray as the head of my house that you keep me in your perfect will. Help me make you the head of my life, Lord.

Thank you being the head of the church. Help me to attend that I may worship you. Allow me to walk in your ways. Move the barriers of my life that I may see and hear from you daily. While I am deployed to another country, be the head of my house for my wife and children. For I am depending on you with all my heart.

My Faith in God: My faith is that God is the head of my house. I will walk in His word and trust Him.

Confess and believe!

Today, I turn my house over to you, Lord, that you may restore and bless it!

CHILDREN OF GOD

*Train up a child in the way he should go: and when he is old,
he will not depart from it. (Proverbs 22:6 KJV)*

Lord, help me ensure all my children are treated special. Help me see their spiritual value. I pray that I can help them shape the future for future generations for the glory of our Lord. I pray that my serving this nation's military or occupation will be an example of shaping the future. I pray most of all that my walk in Christ our Lord will be the highest example. So I need you, Lord, to help me walk uprightly and to be the example of my children. **"Lo children are an heritage of the lord: and the fruit of the womb is his reward"** (Psalm 127:3-5 KJV).

My Faith in God: My faith is that God will train my child and use me as a parent as well to train them in the Lord's holy word.

Confess and believe!

Today, I turn my children over to God. Lord, you have the perfect ways to train my child so that they will be blessed.

GIVE ME A CLEAN HEART

Create in me a clean heart, O God; and renew a right spirit within me. (Psalm 51:10 KJV)

Father, I have a heart that needs to be searched. Sometimes my heart can be a heart of stone. Help me remove the stones from my heart, and may it be open to you and gentle to others.

Create in me a clean heart, O God; and renew a right spirit within me. Lord, help my thoughts to be peaceful and full of harmony. Lord, when my heart is hardened because of war in a foreign land or against anyone, I come before you and ask you to cleanse my heart and remove its hardness and my sinful ways.

I ask that you restore a right spirit within me. Even with the turmoil of my enemy firing and setting up ambushes against me daily, help my heart not to be filled with evil but to be pleasing in your sight, Lord. In the name of Jesus Christ, amen.

My Faith in God: I have faith that God will renew a right Sprit in inside me.

Confess and believe!

Today, I submit myself to you Lord because you have power to help me clean up my acts.

NOT FORGOTTEN

If I regard iniquity in my heart, the Lord will not hear me:
But verily God hath heard me; he hath attended to the voice
of my prayer. (Psalm 66:18-19 KJV)

Lord, thank you for not forgetting about me. Thank you for never leaving me or forsaking me.

Lord, help me pray without iniquity in my heart. Cleanse my heart; purge me by your power, Father. Hear my prayers, Father, and answer according to your loving kindness and purpose for my life. If I have anything against any friends, brothers, or anyone at all, cleanse me and change my heart and attitude that it may be pleasing in your sight. I pray to become a faithful witness for your kingdom. Help me to not have iniquity in my heart against family and friends. Restore me where I need it. Thank you for showing me the power of your love and forgiveness

Thank you for the example you revealed through Joseph's life when his brothers had put him in a pit, and he was sold into slavery. Yet because he trusted you and did not hold iniquity in his heart, you blessed him, Lord. Praise to your name, Jesus.

My Faith in God: My faith is that God has cleansed my heart and made me righteous.

Confess and believe!

Today, I turn my heart over to you, Lord. Please continue to guide me in the right direction.

FORGIVENESS

For if ye forgive men their trespasses, your heavenly Father will also forgive you: But if ye forgive not men their trespasses, neither will your Father forgive your trespasses. (Matthew 6:14-15)

Lord, help me forgive anyone who has trespassed against me. Help me allow that spirit of forgiveness for family, friends, and fellow soldiers. Help other people to forgive each those that need forgiveness. for past, present and future mess-ups.

Father, you said if I forgive men their trespasses, you will also forgive me of my trespasses. But if I do not forgive men their trespasses, neither will you forgive my trespasses. Help me not to dig up the past faults of anyone. Lord, help me in the heat of battle in Iraq and Afghanistan, when I have hurt someone.

Change my ways when I have sinned in your sight. Help me with my tongue in avoiding unpleasant words that are harmful and hurtful to my family neighbors, brothers, sisters and my combat team in battle. Help me to avoid placing curses and scares with my words on my brother, but rather place blessings and forgiveness with my words to improve and establish new relationships with my family and friends.

Lord, if I have said anything that was not pleasant in your sight, forgive me now. In the blessed name of our Lord, Jesus Christ, amen.

My Faith in God: I use my faith to forgive everyone including my enemies. Faith in God is the only way to let that hurt and pain go!

Confess and believe!

Today, I turn my heart over to you, Lord, so that my forgiveness will be real and meaningful.

GRACE

For by grace are ye saved through faith; and that not of yourselves: it is the gift of God: not of works, lest any man should boast. For we are his workmanship, created in Christ Jesus unto good works, which God hath before ordained that we should walk in them. (Ephesians 2:8-10 KJV)

Father, I thank you for your grace. Your grace is purely your love and unmerited favor in my life. Without your grace, I would not be alive.

Lord, I now know that it was your grace alone that saved me. You saved me from the wrath that your Father in heaven could have poured out on me for my sin. But Father, you in your forever tender love and kindness sent your Son, Jesus, to take my place and then offer salvation to me. I thank you that while I serve in the armed forces of America, and wherever I go in this world, I will remember your grace. I will remember that Jesus came to the earth full of grace and truth.

I accept you as my Lord and Savior because I believe that your Son, Jesus, died on the cross and rose from the dead with all power in His hand. Now He sits at your right hand in heaven. I praise you and give you honor and glory forever and ever, in Jesus's name, amen.

My Faith in God: I use my faith to walk in unmerited favor from Jesus Christ that I never deserved.

Confess and believe!

Today, I receive underserved favor in my life from Jesus Christ. I believe that favor is all over my life and will not get away. It is permanent favor!

JUSTIFICATION

Therefore being justified by faith, we have peace with God through our Lord Jesus Christ: by whom also we have access by faith into this grace wherein we stand, and rejoice in hope of the glory of God. (Romans 5:1-2)

Father, thank you for taking away the guilt that I felt in my life. Thank you that, through Jesus, we are justified by faith and that we have access into His grace. Thank you that even when guilt seems to want to return, I can solely depend on you to remove the guilt that I may encounter.

When your disciple Peter felt guilt after he betrayed you, you forgave him and still allowed him to minister to your people. Even while I serve this nation in the armed forces help me to tell about how you justified us through your blood and your love. Thank you for the grace you have made given us. In Jesus's name, amen.

My Faith in God: I use my faith to walk with a justified spirit. I walk free without guilt because of the Son of God. He has set me free from all sin.

Confess and believe!

Today I confess and receive my freedom from and in Jesus Christ!

HEALING

He healeth the broken in heart, and bindeth up their wounds. (Psalm 147:3 KJV)

Lord, I was deployed to war during Operation Iraqi Freedom and the Afghanistan campaign. Father, I was wounded in many ways. I lost part of me in that war. Help me through the moments in my life when my wounds try to get the best of me. Help me when they try to discourage me. Help me when my mind is attacked and I feel at the lowest in my life.

I ask you, Lord, to help me with my wounds when difficult moments arise even in my rehabilitation care. I need you to carry me daily when my heart aches because of the reminders or the pain of my wound. Strengthen my faith in you, Lord, as I go about my daily business at home or wherever I am throughout the day. I need you to heal my injuries and scars daily. Walk with me and talk to me every moment of the day, Lord.

Lord, I ask that you renew me in your spirit because the enemy tries constantly to resurface things in order to bring me low and one his casualties. You are my source of strength. You are my shield and buckler. You are the tender love I need each and every day. Walk with me daily, Lord.

Be my strength. Healing comes from your everlasting love and care. I am reminded even in your word in Isaiah 53:5, you said, "But He was wounded for our transgressions, He was bruised for our iniquities; the chastisement for our peace was upon Him, and by His stripes we are healed" Isaiah 53:5(NKJV).

I now know that I have you to walk with me daily. Today, I will lean on you with all of my wounds, emotional, physical, and spiritual hurt. I surrender my heart problems and every waking day of my life to you, Father, that I may be ever in your presence. I thank you that you are the God of healing and the God who has given me your unfailing, faithful compassion during my time of despair and loneliness. No one can take the place of your touch, your love and kindness. In your holy and precious name, Jesus, amen.

My Faith in God: I use my faith for my heart to be healed and when my spirit has been attacked or broken.

Confess and believe!

Today I confess and receive my healing in Jesus Christ!

VETERANS

I have fought a good fight, I have finished my course, I have kept the faith: henceforth there is laid up for me a crown of righteousness, which the Lord, the righteous judge, shall give me at that day: and not to me only, but unto all them also that love his appearing. (2 Timothy 4:7-8 KJV)

Lord, thank for giving me the faith that I needed to serve and retire from the armed forces. I fought a good fight. I thank you for strength. Thank you for guiding me through the years of deployments and war. You watched over me countless times during challenging and multiple missions and difficulty with my family. You sheltered me under your arm of protection when I was not aware of it.

You loved me when I needed you most. You loved me even when I did not know the meaning of true love. You loved me when I did not love you back. Now you are guiding me again but this time through my retirement years. Lord, I fought a good fight the best I knew how in the military. I pray to fight a good fight serving you as a witness to the world. Grant me the strength and wisdom.

Lord, I thank you with every ounce of my heart and soul for giving the ability to serve and fight with faith. I ask now that you allow me to serve you throughout the remainder of my years. Allow me to finish the race under the power of the Holy Spirit in faith. You know what abilities and gifts that I possess. Use this temple of clay and while you use me continue to heal me where I am broken. Help me to use my basic skills learned in the armed forces for the uplifting of your kingdom. You are worthy of all glory and honor and thanksgiving. Even on my last leg stand and last breath, I desire to give you praise with my soul, heart, and spirit as I open my lips and speak your word and your name in adoration. In Jesus's name, amen.

My Faith in God: My faith is that I will receive a crown in Jesus's name because I fought the good fight and finished the course that He laid out for me.

Confess and believe!

Today, I confess and receive my blessing as a veteran in the armed forces of America and in God's Army.

SALVATION

That if thou shalt confess with thy mouth the Lord Jesus, and shalt believe in thine heart that God hath raised him from the dead, thou shalt be saved. (Romans 10:9 KJV)

Heavenly father, I ask that you grant me eternal life. I never truly understood the power of your resurrection. Today, I have learned more about your word and your magnificence. I confess that Jesus is the son of god and god raised him from the dead. I ask you lord to come into my heart and be my personal savoir. I accept you as my lord and Savior. I repent and ask you Lord for forgiveness of my sin. Thank you Lord for coming into my heart. I am eternally thankful for being the sacrificial lamb of God. Thank you for dying on the cross for my sin. I love you Lord, I adore you and praise your holy name. Lord, also ask that you walk with me daily while I take this new step in my life in the spirit during my job in the military, all events and at all time.

My Faith in God: My faith is that I Jesus died and rose from the dead because He loved me then and loves me now. He also wants me live with him eternally.

Confess and believe!

Today, I confess and receive my blessing of eternal life and the blessing you to walk in it.

HOLY, HOLY, HOLY

In the year that king Uzziah died I saw also the Lord sitting upon a throne, high and lifted up, and his train filled the temple. Above it stood the seraphims: each one had six wings; with twain he covered his face, and with twain he covered his feet, and with twain he did fly. And one cried unto another, and said, Holy, holy, holy, is the Lord of hosts: the whole earth is full of his glory. (Isaiah 6:1-3 KJV)

Thanks be to you, Lord Almighty. I recognize your holiness as best I can. "Holy, holy, holy" comes from my lips to you, Father. Isaiah saw you high and lifted up on the day he was called as a prophet. I pray to be transformed today to see you as he saw you at that moment of his life. You are holy, and you are the saving God with your grace and loving kindness. Father, I need your Holy Spirit to guide me in worship and reverence with your angels and prophets and all your children. I bow before you with all adoration, praise, and worship. Holy, holy, holy. Help me become a partaker of your holiness, and let your Spirit take root in me, to fashion me according to your purpose and will. Lord, if you would be so kind as to allow your newly transformed servant to shout, "Holy, holy, holy!" in the midst of military deployments to Iraq and Afghanistan, and during overseas tour of duty assignments. In the blessed name of Jesus I pray, amen.

My Faith in God: My faith helps my tongue to speak, "Holy, holy, holy," so that I will glorify Him.

Confess and believe!

Today I confess giving God all the glory, for He is the only true and wise God. Holy, holy, holy is the name of Jesus Christ. We must recognize His awesome goodness.

SANCTIFICATION

For they that are after the flesh do mind the things of the flesh;
but they that are after the Spirit the things of the Spirit. For
to be carnally minded is death; but to be spiritually minded
is life and peace. (Romans 8:5-6 KJV)

Thank you, Lord Jesus, that you help me take my life to a new level. Lord, as I serve this nation in combat zones and at home, help me change to reflect a spiritual life in Jesus Christ. Father, create in me a transformed mind to know you and the power and substance that you provide in my life. Help me become a partaker of your holiness, and let your Spirit take root in me to fashion me according to your purpose and will. Lord, if you would be so kind as to allow your newly transformed servant to witness even as I serve the military on deployments to Iraq and Afghanistan and during overseas tour of duty assignments. In the blessed name of Jesus I pray, amen.

My Faith in God: My faith helps me concentrate on the things of the Spirit. I need God to keep my focus on godly things and on pleasing God. My family needs me more than I know.

Confess and believe!

Today I confess giving God all the glory, for He is the only true and wise God, Holy, holy, holy is the name of Jesus Christ. We must recognize His awesome goodness.

MY SOUL

As the deer pants for the water brooks, so pants my soul for You, O God, My soul thirsts for God, for the living God. (Psalm 42:1-2)

Heavenly Father, sometimes I feel a deep void within me that I am unable to describe. Lord, I do realize that I have an empty place in my heart which affects my life. The deer searches out with deep desire the water that helps to sustain life. If he does not find it, he will die. So will the man who never finds God. If he finds Him, he will live, because God is the God who gives new life.

Some men thirst for so many things in life and never find that which fulfills their desires. Some men thirst to sit in the highest position of authority. Some men thirst to have all the riches in the world. Millions and billions of dollars can be at your feet, and you can still have a thirst that you have not acknowledged.

Something tells me that my soul thirsts for you, Sovereign Lord, even in the heat of battle. It is that empty space that affects me with a sense of longing for you. My belief has been in everything around me, idol gods, and things made by man. Now that I have discovered you, Lord, touch my soul with your mighty hand. I ask you to come into my life and fill the void and cover me. Keep me in your righteousness. Thank you, Lord, that you quenched my thirst for you. I ask that every time I thirst—and even if I drift away. Remind me that you are the one who quenches my thirst and restores my soul. My soul belongs to you as I present myself to you, Lord.

> **My Faith in God: My faith helps me to seek God to fill my thirst when I feel empty, lonely, confused, or lost. I desire that you fill me with your love, Lord Jesus Christ.**

Confess and believe!

Today, I confess giving God all the glory, for He is the only true and wise God, Holy, holy, holy is the name of Jesus Christ. We must recognize his awesome goodness.

TEMPTATION

It is written, "Man shall not live by bread alone, but by every word that proceeds out of the mouth of God." (Matthew 4:4)

Lord, in your prayer you said, "Lead us not into temptation, but deliver us from evil." Father, help me in the times on deployment when I get tempted to indulge my fleshly desires. Help me avoid those who try to lower me into temptations of sin. Guard me against demons that prey after my soul and my life.

Jesus said to the enemy, "It is written, thou shall not tempt the Lord thy God," because the enemy tried to tempt Him to turn stones into bread. He also offered Jesus all kingdoms, which really means everything, if He would bow down and worship him. The enemy is deceptive and yet bold in convincing people to obey him.

Sadly, there are some who bow to the enemy. Christians must help them recover. The enemy has no truth, only lies and manipulation. But God is the truth and the way and the life. God is the word of truth and life, and He makes everything good. God is the bread of life. Father, keep us from temptation, and help us meditate on your written word of life. In Jesus's name, amen.

My Faith in God: My faith helps me seek God to get through times of temptation. I will call on the name of Jesus Christ.

Confess and believe!

Today, I confess giving God all the glory for delivering me and saving from giving in to temptation. My marriage is still alive because of God.

PURPOSE

And we know that all things work together for good to them that love God, to them who are the called according to his purpose. (Romans 8:28 KJV)

Father, there are times in my life when I do not understand why things happen; your love brings me through. Thank you for your word, which says all things work for the good of those who are called according to your purpose. Thank you for demonstrating a love so holy, even when I turn my back on you, you always make me feel I am somebody and have self-worth.

Thank you that your love extends beyond my imagination and has no limits. Even in my most complicated, depressed, and confused times of military service, you extended your hand of love that filled and conquered my emptiness, pain, and doubt. In your love and kindness, you even revealed to me my purpose as a child of the Most High God. Lord,

I thank you that you worked out every moment of my military career. I am thankful to be a Christian and a soldier used by you, Lord, even during battles and throughout my career. You made it work for your purpose. Therefore, I must glorify you at all times. In Jesus's name, amen.

> **My Faith in God: My faith helps me walk in my purpose. God called me to serve and He will work it out as long as I am obedient.**

Confess and believe!

Today, I confess giving God all the glory, because He has delivered me through times of temptation that could have destroyed my life. Holy, holy, holy is the name of Jesus Christ. We must recognize His awesome goodness.

REPENT

Repent therefore and be converted, that your sins may be blotted out, so that times of refreshing may come from the presence of the Lord, and that He may send Jesus Christ, who was preached to you before, whom heaven must receive until the times of restoration of all things, which God has spoken by the mouth of all of His holy prophets since the world began. (Acts 3:19-21)

Lord, you said that no one knows the day or the hour of your return. Nevertheless, in your word you tell all people to repent. Repent means to turn your life around—to go in the opposite direction, away from the trouble and sin that distracts you and hunts you down.

May every man present himself before you, Lord, even in his worst condition. Lord, I come to you, Jesus, to repent of my sinful ways. Lord, change my heart to turn from my old ways to you. I pray, Father, that while I am in the military and on my assignment, you will help me turn away from my sinful ways. I desire to obey you at this very moment because you commanded that all men, regardless of where they are, come to repent.

I ask that you help me walk in my new way of life. Empower me with your Holy Spirit, Lord, that I may be pleasing in your sight. Keep me that I may be fit for your kingdom on earth as a witness to all people.

Lord, I accept you as my Lord and Savior in my heart right now! I repent of my sins. Lord, I believe that you died on the cross and were raised from the dead and washed my sins away. You gave me new life in the spirit. In Jesus's name, amen.

My Faith in God: My faith helps me seek God for repentance so my life will be turned around. I desire to walk in your will, Lord, and turn from my old lifestyle. In Jesus's name.

Confess and believe!

Today I confess giving all the glory to God, for He recognizes my times of repentance. Thank you, Lord.

BELIEVE IN GOD

For God so loved the world, that He gave His only begotten Son, that whoever believes in Him should not perish but have everlasting life. For God did not send His Son into the world to condemn the world, but that the world through him might be saved.

He who believes in Him is not condemned; but he who does not believe is condemned already, because he has not believed in the name of the only begotten Son of God. (John 3:16-18)

Belief is powerful because it takes your heart to the place that you desire. The bottom line up front is that God wants every man, woman, and child to believe in Him. It is not an option for eternal life. If you want to live with God forever in heaven, you must believe. His love convinces us.

Men believe in thousands of things in this world because they grip their heart. However, none of those things can give or sustain life. Only Jesus Christ can do give life and keep us. It should never be optional to believe in God. Pray this prayer, and believe in God this day:

Father, I believe in you and your Son, Jesus. Help me know and be sure that I believe in my heart. Thank you that you loved me so much and gave your Son so that through the power of your death and resurrection I can live today and not be condemned. I pray, Lord, today that all people may come to believe in the name of the only begotten Son of God, Jesus Christ. I pray that every soldier may take a time out from battle and wars to acknowledge in firm belief that Jesus is the Son of God and give Him all the praise and glory.

My Faith in God: My faith helps me believe in God. As long as I believe in God, my life will be changed, and the path will be different because I know who to go to for help and repentance. In Jesus Christ.

Confess and believe!

Today I confess giving God all the glory, because He helped me believe in Him by His mighty power and wonders.

RESURRECTION

*For I delivered unto you first of all that which I also received,
how that Christ died for our sins according to the scriptures;
and that he was buried, and that he rose again the third day
according to the scriptures: and that he was seen of Cephas,
then of the twelve. (1 Corinthians 15:3-5 KJV)*

The resurrection is God convincing His people of His love for them. He defeated death. Jesus took the sting out of death. Death has no power over us because the life in Jesus Christ prevails over death.

Father, help me rise up from the natural state of being to the spiritual state of life in Jesus Christ. Thank you for proving your power when you raised your Son, Jesus, from the dead. Help me die to the old sin nature; then resurrect and revive me to live in the fullness of your power. Build my marriage and relationship with my wife and children. Lord, help me know you and live in your kingdom forever. Paul prayed in your word that I might know Jesus and the power of His resurrection and the fellowship of His suffering, being conformed to His death—if by any means I might attain to the resurrection of the dead. Lord, may you change me to walk in newness of life in Jesus Christ, my Lord. In the precious name of Jesus, amen.

My Faith in God: My faith in God reminds me each day of the resurrected King of glory, Jesus Christ, who washed my sin away.

Confess and believe!

Today I confess giving God all the glory, for He is the only true and wise God. Holy, holy, holy is the name of Jesus Christ. We must recognize His awesome goodness.

FAITH

Now faith is the substance of things hoped for, the evidence of things not seen. (Hebrews 11:1 KJV)

Father, you said you gave a measure of faith to every man. This means it was not given based on my status in society but based on God's purpose for my life. As a soldier, who travels the ground and sky and on ships in this great military, I need your guidance of faith.

Lord, help me use my faith effectively in moving mountains out of my life. You showed us that God's prophets were great heroes of faith. They had in common their strong commitment and undeniable faith in the Lord Jesus. Help me be a soldier in this army who believes in you with all my heart, so that it will help me also to accomplish my military missions.

Increase my faith to excel in my military occupational skill, whether engineer, infantry, artillery, pilot, chemical, military police, or any specialty. Help me move huge barriers, so that I may generate momentum and achieve superior results at the outcome. In Jesus name, amen.

My Faith in God: My faith grows each day because of the power in Jesus Christ and His love demonstrated.

Confess and believe!

Today I confess that my faith grows because of Jesus Christ.

WORSHIP

God is a Spirit: and they that worship him must worship him in spirit and in truth. (John 4:24 KJV)

God is a spirit and cannot be touched with human hands. Every day His spirit is in heaven and all around us. He awaits true worshippers to get into the Spirit and come before Him with thanksgiving.

Father, thank you for helping me understand that I must worship you in Spirit and in truth. I desire that my worship will completely focus on you, that I may be in your presence and experience your blessings. I never desire anything outside of you, Father. Help me exalt and edify you with all my heart. Lord, I adore you and magnify your precious name for all of your grace and mercy. Lord, grant me to renew my spirit, to be connected with yours daily. Be with me as I deploy to other countries and during my family time as well as military obligations.

Lord, I desire to know your truth each passing day of my life. Keep me on the path of worship by your Holy Spirit.

My Faith in God: My faith helps me walk with wisdom as I count on you, Lord Jesus.

Confess and believe!

Today I confess giving God all the glory, for He is the only true and wise God. Holy, holy, holy is the name of Jesus Christ. We must recognize His awesome goodness.

BORN AGAIN

Jesus answered, Verily, verily, I say unto thee, Except a man be born of water and of the Spirit, he cannot enter into the kingdom of God. (John 3:5 KJV)

Father, thank you for allowing me to make a choice to become born again. Thank you for the power you placed into salvation and baptism. I believe salvation and baptism will help me in my worship life. I believe now that it is relevant for relationship.

You said to Nicodemus that you must be born again. Lord, as I open my heart today; allow it to be receptive to you only. Set my mind to receive what it is you have to tell me. By the power of the Holy Spirit, guide me to the deepest realm of worship so that my soul will magnify you. Transform me and baptize me in the Spirit that I may walk in a sincere relationship with you Lord. In the name of Jesus, amen

My Faith in God: I accepted Jesus as Lord in my life. Now I am born again. My spirit is renewed in Jesus Christ.

Confess and believe!

Today I confess giving God all the glory, for He is the only true and wise God. Holy, holy, holy is the name of Jesus Christ. We must recognize His awesome goodness.

GROWING IN PERFECT GRACE

For by grace are ye saved through faith; and that not of yourselves: it is the gift of God: not of works, lest any man should boast. (Ephesians 2:8-9 KJV)

Lord, thank you for reminding me that I am saved by grace and not by works. Thank you for giving me unmerited favor. I did not earn it, nor do I deserve it. But your perfect and unfailing love is the reason why I am so blessed in your grace.

Thank you for grace when I was deployed in the war zone and made it back to my family. Thank you for grace when I was miserable and sinking in sin. Lord, your grace helped me realize your great compassion, love, and kindness. I exalt you for your grace. Thank you for caring for my fellow comrades, soldiers, friends, team members and leaders in my unit, and other units as well.

Now I know and understand that you can never fail and your grace is of your love for humanity and your people. Thank you for including me and every soldier in the armed forces. Thank you for giving and placing grace over my life.

My Faith in God: It is our faith in Jesus Christ that saves us. We do not save ourselves. The only part is going to church and responding at invitation.

Confess and believe!

Today I confess giving God all the glory, for He is the only true and wise God. Holy, holy, holy is the name of Jesus Christ. We must recognize His awesome goodness.

JESUS IS THE SON OF GOD

Simon Peter answered and said, Thou art the Christ, the Son of the living God. (Matthew 16:16 KJV)

There will be times when Jesus will ask you a question. What will your answer be when someone else asks you who Jesus is? Make sure you answer just like Peter. If you do so, you have answered Jesus as well. You can pass the test. Pray this prayer:

Father, thank you for your Son, Jesus Christ, whom you revealed to Simon Peter as the Son of the living God. Thank you for revealing Him to me today. I know the truth now. Therefore I can give the answer to others who do not know Him.

Thank you for your Son, Jesus, who brought everlasting life to those who accept Him. He came and died on the cross to remove all my sin, all the wrongdoings that I ever committed. Thank you for forgiving me even when I don't forgive myself. Thank you that Jesus is the head of the church, and He awaits those who will accept Him as Lord.

I pray today that the Lord will change me so I can identify my need for Him in my life. Lord, I realize that money and fame will not bless me as you do. So today, I accept you in my heart and in my life. Thank you that you live forever. From now on I can call on the living God through His Son for all things. In Jesus's name, amen.

> **My Faith in God: It takes faith to believe that Jesus is the Son of God. The power you need comes from His word, which is truth.**

> **Confess and believe!**

Today I confess giving God all the glory, for He is the only true and wise God. Holy, holy, holy is the name of Jesus Christ. We must recognize His awesome goodness.

CHURCH

And I also say to you that you are Peter, and on this rock I will build My church, and the gates of Hades shall not prevail against it. (Matthew 16:18)

Lord, thank you for the church and leaders you provide. Thank for the sanctity of the church. You revealed to the Apostle Peter the authority of the church of our Lord Jesus Christ, the anointed one. Thank you, Lord Jesus, for you are our key to heaven, and your presence dwells among us in the sanctuary.

Lord, allow my body to be a sanctuary for your indwelling Help me to be a part of the church, the body of Christ. Lord, enter into my heart while I am in the armed forces, serving my country. Transform my mind and heart and spirit. Lord, touch me wherever I am stationed. Keep me by the power of your Holy Spirit to worship and exalt you, Lord, even in the combat zone.

My Faith in God: My faith is in the head of the church, Jesus Christ.

Confess and believe!

Today I confess giving God all the glory, for He is the only true and wise God. Holy, holy, holy is the name of Jesus Christ. We must recognize His awesome goodness.

LOVE

And now abideth faith, hope, charity, these three; but the greatest of these is charity. (1 Corinthians 13:13 KJV)

If you ask people who are in love with their wife or husband, they would have to tell you that love is the greatest. Love starts with relationships and sustains them. Love reaches to the depths. of our soul, heart, and spirit. Everyone longs for love. Love is a necessity. We pray harder and harder because we want the love of God and love from someone else.

Father, thank you for loving me every time I need it. You gave your love to me so that I can make it through the tough times, the hurtful times, the disappointments in life. You make my life worth living because of your love. I will walk in faith and hope because of your love. Most of all, I need your love to walk as a Christian and to love my family as I should.

It is a requirement for husbands and wives to love one another. It is a requirement for family members to love one another. There should never be a split or division.

You reveal love to me even in combat. I want to thank you for loving me when I arrived back home from Iraq. Praise to your Holy name.

> **My Faith in God: My faith is in you, Jesus, because you always show me love. It is your love that strengthens me. In Jesus Christ's name, amen.**

Confess and believe!

Today I confess giving God all the glory, for He is the only true and wise God. Holy, holy, holy is the name of Jesus Christ. We must recognize His awesome goodness.

MORE THAN CONQUERORS

Who shall separate us from the love of Christ? Shall tribulation, or distress, or persecution, or famine, or nakedness, or peril, or sword? . . . Yet in all these things we are more than conquerors through Him who loved us. (Romans 8:35, 37)

Father, thank you for giving me a spirit to be more than a conqueror. I can stand strong now. Help me, Lord, as I go about my daily duties as a soldier in the United States armed forces. I pray for your Holy Spirit to remind me daily to think and go before you in prayer and thanksgiving before every mission. I pray for obedience to get up in the morning and pray. Lord, I pray an attitude like Daniel to go before you three times a day. Give me patience, humility, and obedience. You are my God, and I will meditate on your word day and night. I pray to abide in your word even when things get tough. I pray to be more than a conqueror because nothing can separate me from the love of Jesus Christ.

My Faith in God: My faith helps me overcome my obstacles because I am more than a conqueror in Jesus Christ.

Confess and believe!

Today I confess giving God all the glory because He gave me courage through tough times.

WARRIOR SPIRIT

And the Angel of the Lord appeared to him, and said to him, "The Lord is with you, you mighty man of valor!" (Judges 6:12)

When I think of a mighty man of valor, I think of someone with a warrior spirit, a warrior attitude—just someone courageous. God is looking for men and women just like that. Ask God for a warrior spirit.

Father, thank you for protecting me and my fellow soldiers in combat. You blessed me through all the raids and patrols, the battles that I faced within the combat zone, Iraq or Afghanistan. Today, I pray for a warrior spirit to reflect the spirit that God gave Gideon. Help me be a man of confidence and faith in you, Lord. You called Gideon a mighty man of valor to reflect his courage and victories to come only through your will. I pray to have like faith and strength only for the uplifting of your kingdom while I am in Iraq or Afghanistan. Lord, send your angel to visit me so that I will stand strong, no matter what. Thank you for giving me strength and enabling me to survive combat. I pray that all soldiers can be warriors who stand for peace and freedom in the Lord our God.

> **My Faith in God: My faith helps me overcome obstacles because I am more than a conqueror in Jesus Christ. A conqueror walks with confidence and strength. Keep your faith!**

Confess and believe!

Today I confess giving God all the glory, for He is the only true and wise God. Holy, holy, holy is the name of Jesus Christ. We must recognize His awesome goodness.

FIGHT FOR YOUR LIFE

Then the Lord said to Gideon, "By the three hundred men who lapped I will save you, and deliver the Midianites into your hand, Let all the other people go, every man to his place." (Judges 7:7)

God knows how to select and whom to select. Lord, thank you for your power of selecting the right men with the right spirit. Lord, as I go out on missions each day, give me the right spirit. Help me in this fight for my life. Remind me of the obedience and faith that you planted in me. Keep my mind on you as my shield and buckler. Remind me that I can look to the hills, from whence cometh my help. My help comes from the living God.

Lord, I pray as a leader and a follower to be in your perfect will. Lord, keep me while I am in this dangerous and unruly combat zone. Send your angels to surround me and your people. I pray for you to be my Lord and comforter forever. Lord, when I finish this mission for the armed forces, I pray to become a soldier in your Army. I pray to tell everyone I know about you dying on the cross for me. I pray by the power of your Holy Spirit to remain in your Army and walk in salvation forever and ever. In Jesus's name, amen.

My Faith in God: My faith helps me fight for my life in Jesus Christ. God wants us to be like the men that stood by the side of Gideon.

Confess and believe!

Today I confess giving God all the glory, for He is the only true and wise God. Holy, holy, holy is the name of Jesus Christ. We must recognize His awesome goodness.

FRUIT OF THE SPIRIT

But the fruit of the Spirit is love, joy, peace, longsuffering, kindness, goodness, faithfulness, gentleness, self-control. (Galatians 5:22-23)

Lord, I will walk in the Spirit daily under God's influence. You distinguished between man's flesh and the fruit of the Spirit. They both war against each other. The power in the fruit of the Spirit is stronger in these spiritual character traits.

Help me overcome the sin that attempts to overtake my flesh. Bring forth love, joy, peace, longsuffering, kindness, goodness, faithfulness, gentleness, temperance inside me that will help me avoid the works of the flesh, which produces evil ways. Guide my steps in the Spirit daily. In Jesus's name, amen.

My Faith in God: Help me display the fruit of the Spirit. The fruit of the Spirit wins souls.

Confess and believe!

Today, I confess that I need the Holy Spirit to demonstrate the fruit of the Spirit.

KEEP YOUR JOY

These things I have spoken to you, that My joy may remain in you, and that your joy may be full. (John 15:11)

The Lord explains to me that His joy inside me fills me and remains in me. Jesus said that it remains in me. Father, thank you for the joy you put inside my heart and spirit. Lord, I am experiencing this joy that is unspeakable. Lord, this joy you gave me helps me express myself differently to other people. I cannot tell it all. Lord, even while I am in a combat zone fighting battles day after day, you fill my heart with joy because you are my Lord who loves me so. Lord, always allow this joy to remain full even in my toughest times on the battlefield, in deployments, and in my life at home-stateside.

James 1:1-3 says, "My brethren, count it all joy when you fall into various trials, knowing that the testing of your faith produces patience." Help my joy remain throughout this life and eternity. Keep my family in perfect joy. Help me laugh and smile with the joy of the Lord reflected in my countenance. I trust in you, Lord, to help me keep my joy. In Jesus's name, amen.

My Faith in God: My faith helps me keep my joy. Do not allow anything or anyone to steal your joy, no matter where you are in the world.

Confess and believe!

Today I confess that giving God all the glory helps me keep my joy. When I am weak, then I am strong because He perfects Himself in weakness.

PEACE OF GOD

And the peace of God, which surpasses all understanding, will guard your hearts and minds through Christ Jesus. (Philippians 4:7)

Peace I leave with you, My peace I give to you; not as the world gives do I give to you. Let not your heart be troubled, neither let it be afraid. (John 14:27)

Father, I thank you that you are the God of peace. I pray peace in my life daily. I pray peace in my home. I pray peace all around us and in the world. I pray peace for those who do not know Jesus Christ as Lord and Redeemer, in Jesus's name.

I thank you for helping me have thoughts of peace in my heart. When troubles hit hard or tragedy strikes the family, I need peace. Thank you, Lord, because when I get weary, you help me maintain peaceful thoughts in my mind and heart. I need your divine peace to sustain my life. You help me and comfort me with peace that surpasses all understanding. Your peace, Lord, gives the surest, deepest harmony and serenity because you care about me.

Nothing can compare to your peace, Lord. Before I go to combat in a foreign land or even at home, let your peace continually cover me and my family. When trials and tribulations, hurtfulness, pain, and loneliness come my way, grant me your peace. Lord, I am forever thankful for your peace. In your precious name, Lord, amen.

> **My Faith in God: My faith helps me have peace of mind, heart, and spirit.**

> **Confess and believe!**

Today I confess giving God all the glory, for He is the only true and wise God. Holy, holy, holy is the name of Jesus Christ. We must recognize His awesome goodness.

SPIRITUAL GROWTH

*By this My Father is glorified, that you bear much fruit; so
you will be My disciples. (John 15:8)*

Lord, I thank you that you will allow me to glorify you. You always deserve
all the glory and honor and thanksgiving, as the elders and angels reveal in
heaven this day and forever more.

Help me by the power of your Holy Spirit to be pleasing in your sight.
Help me grow even in my times of serving this nation in war. Help me be
a fruit bearer even in the worst of conditions and times of disorder. Help
me live displaying the fruit of the Spirit. While I continue to represent this
nation, help me represent the Lord, our sovereign God. My prayer is that
I become a disciple and bear much fruit so that you will be glorified. Help
me serve you in that capacity of ministry. In Jesus's name, amen.

My Faith in God: My faith helps me be a better follower of Jesus Christ.

Confess and believe!

Today I confess giving God all the glory for he deals with faith in the only
true and wise God. Holy, holy, holy is the name of Jesus Christ. We must
recognize His awesome goodness.

SPIRIT FILLED

And do not be drunk with wine, in which is dissipation; but be filled with the Spirit, speaking to one another in psalms and hymns and spiritual songs, singing and making melody in your heart to the Lord, giving thanks always for all things to God the Father in the name of our Lord Jesus Christ, submitting to one another in the fear of God. (Ephesians 5:18-21)

Have you ever sat in a bar and watched the bartender or the man or woman at the bar pour a drink until it overflows? In some cases, people watch wine and the sparkles and bubbles while pouring in fascination and in anticipation to taste it. We used that example in church: pouring water into a cup until it overflows and starts running all over the place.

When you consume alcohol, it can easily make you want more and more until you are full and then you don't know what happened last night. One friend told you that you were another person they had never seen before. Talk to the Lord so he can deliver you from that to getting Spirit filled. It is better than wine and all the alcoholic beverages. The Bible says, "Taste and see that the Lord is good."

Lord, you clearly tell us not to consume wine to become drunk. You remind us that you have something better than wine. Your Spirit will intoxicate me and your people. Lord, my desire is to be filled with the Spirit today. Lord, when you fill me, never take your Holy Spirit from me. Father, I pray to be Spirit filled daily so that I can walk in the Spirit and not give in to lustful things and those things that are not pleasing in your sight. I pray to be Spirit filled, so that I can do what is right instead of things that are sinful and evil. I want to be used, Lord, and help others in time of need by sharing the love of Jesus Christ. I thank you for your word and the power that changed me. In Jesus's name.

My Faith in God: My faith as a Spirit-filled person in Jesus Christ will enable me to sing for the Lord. God helps me be a better follower of Jesus Christ in the Spirit.

Confess and believe!

Today I confess giving God all the glory, for He is the only true and wise God. Holy, holy, holy is the name of Jesus Christ. We must recognize His awesome goodness.

PROSPERITY

This Book of the Law shall not depart from your mouth, but you shall meditate in it day and night, that you may observe to do according to all that is written in it. For then you will make your way prosperous, and then you will have good success. (Joshua 1:8)

I have never heard of anyone who did not enjoy some form of currency, money, or trading object with a value or worth. If God gave it to you, it must be for a purpose.

Father, thank you that I can walk in prosperity as long as I trust in your word. I can walk in prosperity as long as I obey you and act in ways that please you with what you provide. I pray that you guide me in meditating in your word day and night. Your word says, "Blessed is the man who walks not in the counsel of the ungodly, nor stands in the path of sinners, nor sits in the seat of the scornful, But his delight is in the law of the Lord, and in His law he meditates day and night" (Psalm 1:1-2). I pray that you take me to your word when it seems that I am going astray. Keep me in your word that I may walk in success that will glorify you only. In Jesus's name, amen.

> **My Faith in God: My faith helps me know that I can prosper and become a better follower of Jesus Christ. Riches do not rule my life. Jesus Christ rules my life in every way.**

Confess and believe!

Today I confess giving God all the glory, for He is the only true and wise God. Holy, holy, holy is the name of Jesus Christ. We must recognize His awesome goodness.

GRACE AND GLORY

For the Lord God is a sun and shield: the Lord will give grace and glory: no good thing will he withhold from them that walk uprightly. (Psalm 84:11 KJV)

Father, I exalt your name for giving grace and glory to your people. For this I magnify you with all my heart. I know whom I can depend on in this world. It is you, my Lord Jesus. Lord, help me walk under the control of your Holy Spirit.

I pray to be born again. I pray that my entire household become born again. They need to know how serious I am about Jesus. I pray to be the righteousness of Jesus Christ according to your word, Lord. Thank you for getting me through combat. You brought me home and helped me recover. All the praise to you, in Jesus's name, amen.

My Faith In God: My faith assures me that He will not withhold any good thing.

Confess and believe!

Today I confess giving God all the glory, for He is the only true and wise God. Holy, holy, holy is the name of Jesus Christ. We must recognize His awesome goodness.

RELATIONSHIP

There is therefore now no condemnation to those who are in Christ Jesus, who do not walk according to the flesh, but according to the Spirit. For the law of the Spirit of life in Christ Jesus has made me free from the law of sin and death. For what the law could not do in that it was weak through the flesh, God did by sending His own Son in the likeness of sinful flesh, on account of sin: He condemned sin in the flesh . . . (Romans 8:1-3)

Lord, today I ask to have a relationship with you. My life has been in a state of confusion. Help me overcome feeling condemnation.

Lord, a friend of mine told me that I needed to accept you as Lord to get rid of this condemnation feeling. I surrender today. I accept you as Lord in my life. For too long, I have experienced an identity crisis. It seems sometimes that my friends turn against me. It seems sometimes that life is a challenge which forces me to turn away. When I experience a snare in my life, I believe God is speaking to me in His own way.

I know you gave me life and life is worth living. Life is worth living for many reasons. The primary reason life is worth living is because of you, Lord. I pray to have a deeper relationship with you. Help me avoid distractions in my life that hinder my relationship. I pray that the Holy Spirit remove those things immediately and put me on firm ground. Lord, help me by your Holy Spirit to keep meditating on you. Lord, I pray to be in your presence.

My Faith in God: My faith helps me walk without condemnation. However, I walk in the love of Jesus Christ because He saved me.

Confess and believe!

Today I confess giving God all the glory because He does not condemn me; instead He loves me.

SEEKING GOD

*But seek first the kingdom of God and His righteousness,
and all these things shall be added to you. (Matthew 6:33)*

Lord you know the condition of my heart. I need you to help me seek you with a clear heart and mind. Place in my heart the ambition to seek you first before all things. Guide me by the power of your Holy Spirit. Help me walk in the light of your marvelous ways so that I will reflect that I am a child of the most high God. Be with me even on the battlefield as I serve the armed forces of America. Lord, as you help me understand you more, help me believe and confess you as my Lord and Savior.

> **My Faith in God: My faith helps me seek God to fill my thirst when I feel empty, lonely, confused, or lost. I desire that you fill me with your love, Lord Jesus Christ.**

Confess and believe!

Today I confess giving God all the glory, for He is the only true and wise God. Holy, holy, holy is the name of Jesus Christ. We must recognize His awesome goodness.

YOU CAN FIND GOD!

As for you, my son Solomon, know the God of your father, and serve Him with a loyal heart and with a willing mind; for the Lord searches all hearts and understands all the intent of the thoughts. If you seek Him, He will be found by you; but if you forsake Him, He will cast you off forever. (1 Chronicles 28:9)

Serving God is an honor. You can find God if you look closely enough for Him. When you find God, you will discover that there are blessings involved in serving God with a loyal heart. A loyal heart honors the person to whom loyalty is directed.

Lord, you always make yourself available for me and everyone else. You never let me down. I desire to know you with all my heart, because you are God, and you keep on blessing me. I desire to have a willing mind to be fixed on you at all times. Help me be the kind of person and soldier who will never turn my back on you, Lord Jesus. I pray that my soul, heart, mind, and strength are yours. You have delivered me even on the battlefield and after I return home. You helped me make through the improvised explosive devices all around me. You even helped me when hatred and violence escalated. I will tell every soldier I know that they can find you, Father, on the battlefield, in the tactical operations center, in the barracks, and at home back stateside. I praise your name, Lord, in Jesus's name.

My Faith in God: My faith helps me seek and find God every time I go to Him.

Confess and believe!

Today I confess giving God all the glory, for He is the only true and wise God. Holy, holy, holy is the name of Jesus Christ. We must recognize His awesome goodness.

118

THANKFULNESS

Be anxious for nothing, but in everything by prayer and supplication, with thanksgiving, let your requests be made known to God. (Philippians 4:6)

Father, thank you for keep my mind settled. Thank you for settling my heart so that I don't worry about things only you can fix. Thank you for my keeping my life daily and providing for me.

Lord, I ask prayers for all soldiers in combat throughout the world. I ask that you help all the saints pray for a breakthrough for the lives of all soldiers. Lord, search every soldier's heart and bring them all closer to you. I pray that you bring soldiers home. Lord, thank you for helping their families, and remind them of your everlasting love. I ask for peace in our hearts, mind, souls, and throughout the world to protect us in war. We pray that war ceases. Thank you, Lord, that you control all things and that you answer prayers according to your will.

My Faith in God: My faith helps me seek God and not worry. I am thankful that you keep my mind and soul intact.

Confess and believe!

Today I confess giving God all the glory for he is the only true and wise God. Holy, holy, holy to my Lord Jesus Christ.

TRANSFORMATION TIME

I beseech you therefore, brethren, by the mercies of God, that you present your bodies a living sacrifice, holy, acceptable to God, which is your reasonable service. (Romans 12:1)

Lord, I present myself to you as a living sacrifice. I understand that you are the God of the living and not the dead. You require a living sacrifice because you are full of life.

Lord, I understand I must become a child of God. A man must become a man of God. A woman must become a woman of God. Thank you for inspiring me to be transformed by the renewing of my mind. It is my time to be transformed. I will not let anything stop me from receiving you as Lord of my life. I will not allow anything to stop me from being transformed today.

Because I understand that this transformation is a metamorphosis process, I will stop in my tracks right now and accept you, Lord Jesus, into my heart. I desire to change from my old ways and be empowered by you. In your word you said, "Ask, and it will be given to you; seek, and you will find; knock, and the door will be opened" (KJV) Matthew 7:7. I thank you, Lord, that you bless me in the military as a soldier and leader by transforming my mind. I will take this personally for the rest of my life. My prayer is that you continue to watch over me during my walk with you as a Christian. I pray for my fellow soldiers and friends to be transformed. In Jesus, name, amen.

My Faith in God: My faith helps me walk in my transformation. I am a new person in Jesus Christ. I will continue to seek Him for strength and love.

Confess and believe!

Today I confess giving God all the glory for transforming my life. He helps me to walk as a man of God.

HIGH PRIEST

Seeing then that we have a great High Priest who has passed through the heavens, Jesus the Son of God, let us hold fast our confession. (Hebrews 4:14)

Father, thank you for sending your Son, Jesus Christ, to save my life. You sent Him to be my High Priest for life. He is the High Priest of heaven and earth. He has all authority in His hand. He protects and guides my life. Your word says, "Seeing then that we have a great high priest, that is passed into the heavens, Jesus the Son of God, let us hold fast our profession" (KJV). You remind us that Jesus felt the pain and hurt that we all have experienced. He has experienced our feelings of infirmities. He was "in all points tempted like as we are, yet without sin" (verse 15).

Thank you that your Holy Spirit is my intercessor in prayer for the betterment of my life. Lord, you said, "Let us therefore come boldly to the throne of grace, that we may obtain mercy and find grace to help in time of need" (verse 16). You said everyone must come through the Son to get to the Father. Help me approach you with boldness daily because I need you daily.

> **My Faith in God: My faith helps me know my High Priest, Jesus Christ. There is no one like Him.**

Confess and believe!

Today I confess giving God all the glory because he is my High Priest. I glorify Him because has defeated the enemy.

Speak It into Existence and Abundance

Then Elijah said to Ahab, "Go get something to eat and drink, for I hear a mighty rainstorm coming!"

So Ahab went to eat and drink. But Elijah climbed to the top of Mount Carmel and bowed low to the ground and prayed with his face between his knees.

Then he said to his servant, "Go and look out toward the sea."

The servant went and looked, then returned to Elijah and said, "I didn't see anything."

Seven times Elijah told him to go and look. Finally the seventh time, his servant told him, "I saw a little cloud about the size of a man's hand rising from the sea."

Then Elijah shouted, "Hurry to Ahab and tell him, 'Climb into your chariot and go back home. If you don't hurry, the rain will stop you!'"

And soon the sky was black with clouds. A heavy wind brought a terrific rainstorm, and Ahab left quickly for Jezreel. Then the Lord gave special strength to Elijah. He tucked his cloak into his belt and ran ahead of Ahab's chariot all the way to the entrance of Jezreel. (1 Kings 18:41-46 NLT)

Father, you always bless me in abundance. When I get back home as well as now, I am looking for blessings in abundance. I am not settling for less in my life, because you gave me the faith to expect abundance. So Lord while I am deployed fighting battles that only you can win, I am keeping my faith in you. I believe that you will see me through.

Now Lord, I am praying for abundance like Elijah prayed for rain. After three and a half years of drought, Elijah prayed, and the abundance of rain flowed in the country and in his life. It was the power of God's word spoken by Elijah that manifested itself to bless his people. Lord, your power and Spirit are more powerful than the rain covering my spirit. Help me follow the example of Elijah and yourself, Lord, to be creator of my words so that you will be glorified. Help me to walk in unity. I pray, Lord, to walk in the best of faith and be filled by your Spirit

My Faith in God: My faith helps me speak things into existence with God's blessing.

Confess and believe!

Today I confess giving God all the glory, for He is the only true and wise God. Holy, holy, holy is the name of Jesus Christ. We must recognize His awesome goodness.

ROYAL PRIESTHOOD

You are a chosen generation, a royal priesthood, a holy nation, His own special people, that you may proclaim the praises of Him who called you out of darkness into His marvelous light; who once were not a people but are now the people of God, who had not obtained mercy but now have obtained mercy. (1 Peter 2:9-10)

Father, you said that I am of the chosen generation, a royal priesthood, and a holy nation—your own special people, that I may proclaim the praises of the One who called me out of darkness into your marvelous light. We once were not a people but now are the people of God.

Lord, help me to live out my identity in priesthood with you. Lord, even when I am deployed, let me never fall away from you, and keep my family in the faith in Jesus Christ. Help me encourage others among my family and friends to come into relationship with you. Thank you for calling me special. Lord, help me to lay aside all malice, deceit, hypocrisy, and all evil speaking that I may grow in your word and walk in priesthood.

My Faith in God: My faith helps me walk as a royal priest of God.

Confess and believe!

Today I confess giving God all the glory, for He is the only true and wise God who made me a royal priest in His kingdom.

PREACH THE WORD!

Preach the word! Be ready in season and out of season. Convince, rebuke, exhort, with all longsuffering and teaching. (2 Timothy 4:2)

When you feel life is draining you and the fire is no longer there, go back to the Lord and ask Him to renew your strength. The enemy, negative thoughts, and some people may get into your head, but stand firm in Jesus Christ. You have to remember that you are like prey to the enemy. Get your head up, rebuke the devil, and call on the name above every name, Jesus Christ, to help you get out of that pit and slump.

Even when you feel life has taken its toll on you and the ministry, you need to remember what Paul told Timothy. He simply said, "Preach the word in season and out of season." In other words, do not let anything, not even time, stop you from being a witness for Jesus Christ. Preach the word! Don't give in to anything! Do not give up on God. God has your back! Preach with backbone! Preach in the Spirit! Preach because God called you to preach. Just preach, Preacher!

God is still in control of everything! If anybody tells you different, it is not the truth. Jesus is the truth! His power is more far-reaching than the mind can comprehend. All kinds of challenges will come, but you have to preach anyway in Jesus's name!

Lord, help me. I am a man of God in the United States armed forces, and I am on the battlefield fighting against terrorism to maintain freedom. I am a preacher, and I need your help. I was called to the ministry, but I am on the battlefield, in a crazy place with crazy people, about to lose my mind. Also about to lose my ministry. Help me be steadfast in preaching the gospel of Jesus Christ even in Iraq, Afghanistan, or any deployment where I might be sent. Give me, through your power and will, the courage and the strength to preach the word in season and out of season, that the word of God might have the effect of a two-edged sword, penetrating the division of soul and spirit. I will preach now because of your strength in my life, Lord Jesus. In Jesus's name, amen.

My Faith in God: My faith helps me preach the word about Jesus Christ.

Confess and believe!

Today I confess giving God all the glory, for He is the only true and wise God. Holy, holy, holy is the name of Jesus Christ. We must recognize His awesome goodness.

A PRAYER OF FAITH SAVES

And the prayer of faith will save the sick, and the Lord will raise him up. (James 5:15)

What are you sick about today? What has you down and out? A prayer of faith saves.

Father, thank you for the prayer of faith. You said that "the prayer of faith will save the sick, and the Lord will raise him up." This prayer is for those who will pray daily by faith for healing of the sick. My prayer is with thanksgiving unto you, Lord, that my request is known to you.

Lord, visit those that seek you and those who have no understanding of you. Visit prisons, battlefields, and hospitals where tragedy and devastating has peaked today and yesterday. Visit the broken homes where families live in constant despair and brokenness. You said, "The effectual fervent prayer of a righteous man availeth much" (James 5:16 KJV).

My Faith in God: My faith helps me in praying for others for healing in Jesus Christ.

Confess and believe!

Today I confess giving God all the glory, for He is the only true and wise God. Holy, holy, holy is the name of Jesus Christ. We must recognize His awesome goodness.

TRAIN YOUR CHILD

Train up a child in the way he should go, and when he is old he will not depart from it. (Proverbs 22:6)

And you, fathers, do not provoke your children to wrath, but bring them up in the training and admonition of the Lord. (Ephesians 6:4)

Father, you always give us patience. Today, I ask for you to help me to train up this child. Thank you because you help us love our families. Thank you for children to love. You blessed me and my children. I realize that as a soldier in the armed forces, I ask that you help me train my children under your influence. Lead me by the power of the Holy Spirit as I continue teaching my children what is right in life. Lord, while I am away help me call back to communicate through your word teachings that will transform my children and enable them to live the best life possible. All praise to your Holy name, amen.

My Faith in God: My faith helps me train my child in your word.

Confess and believe!

Today I confess giving God all the glory, for He is the only true and wise God. Holy, holy, holy is the name of Jesus Christ. We must recognize His awesome goodness.

WAR

In this manner, therefore, pray: Our Father in heaven, hallowed be Your name. Your kingdom come. Your will be done on earth as it is in heaven. Give us this day our daily bread. And forgive us our debts, as we forgive our debtors, And do not lead us into temptation, but deliver us from the evil one. For Yours is the kingdom and the power and the glory forever. Amen. (Matthew 6:9-13)

What soldiers need now more than ever before is to adopt a prayer lifestyle. Soldiers and their families need to change their lives into being prayer warriors. Pray to the Lord in heaven, and let your requests be known. He will deliver according to His will and purpose for you.

Soldiers and their families need to believe in the power of prayer. It is prayer that will hold things together. Prayer will save the soul. Prayer will deliver and help your spirit. Prayer will lift you up every time if you trust in Jesus. You need prayer to call on Jesus to send you guardian angels. Pray for protection. In Psalm 91:11, God said, "I will give my angels charge over you, to keep you in all your ways." What a blessing to know that God will do this holy thing for you and me.

Prayer to protect our troops from defeat: All the saints should be praying to protect the 30,000 or 60,000 soldiers deployed to Afghanistan. Pray for peace and protection and for the families affected by this deployment. Pray that the power of love reaches out in the midst of war. God will surprise you with the things He alone can do.

During this time of war, every soldier needs to pray for a deeper, more intimate relationship with our Father in Heaven. Pray for salvation. Pray for deliverance from any troubles, bondage, or addictions. Pray for what you need Jesus to answer in your life. If you want a relationship, accept Jesus as Lord and Savior in your life. Just say, "Lord Jesus, forgive me of my sin. I repent of my sin! I believe that you are the Son of God. I believe that you died on the cross and were raised from the grave on the third day for the remission of my sin." You have just confessed to the Lord (see

Romans 10:9). You are saved, reborn into the kingdom of God. You are a new creature in Christ Jesus. The old person has gone. Start reading your holy Bible daily, and trust Jesus. His Holy Spirit will guide you all the days of your life.

My Faith in God: My faith helps me to teach and to pray.

Confess and believe!

Today I confess giving God all the glory, for He is the only true and wise God. Holy, holy, holy is the name of Jesus Christ. We must recognize His awesome goodness.

ACCOUNTABILITY

The soul who sins shall die. The son shall not bear the guilt of the father, nor the father bear the guilt of the son. The righteousness of the righteous shall be upon himself, and the wickedness of the wicked shall be upon himself. (Ezekiel 18:20)

Lord, help me be more accountable, caring, and understanding of my own actions. Give me the knowledge to discern right from wrong, that I may be pleasing in your sight. Thank you for reminding me even while I am in combat to tell my family that I love them and for being the God who shelters and protects each person daily. I ask you to help me by the power of the Holy Spirit to be responsible for my own soul and not my family members.

I need you, Lord, to shelter each soul of my family member because I do not have the power, but you have all power Lord in the palm of your hand. I surrender them to you. You have a way of reminding each of us that we are individually responsible for our own souls. Teach us continually the prayer of forgiveness. Take me and my family back to the basics of prayer in Matthew 6:9-13. Teach my son and daughter, and generations to come, that each one them is individually responsible for his or her own actions. Send your power down through the generations to come with blessing into their lives.

My Faith in God: My faith helps keep me accountable to you Lord and my love ones.

Confess and believe!

Today I confess giving God all the glory, for He is the only true and wise God. Holy, holy, holy is the name of Jesus Christ. We must recognize His awesome goodness.

ORDER MY STEPS, LORD

Blessed is the man who walks not in the counsel of the ungodly, nor stands in the path of the sinners, nor sits in the seat of the scornful; but his delight is in the law of the Lord, and in His law he meditates day and night. (Psalm 1:1-2)

Lord, each day I stepped onto the battlefield to accomplish my mission, life seemed surreal. It can be almost like a dream at times that I am truly in the midst of a battle for reasons beyond my control.

Because the days and nights seem so endless, Lord, I ask that you order my steps each day and night. I count it joy because you are able to do anything but fail. I believe that you have the power to order the steps of men and women throughout the world and in the armed forces. Lord, you ordered the steps of your disciples. You ordered the Apostle Peter's steps when he stepped out of the boat onto water to come to you. You ordered the Apostle Paul's steps when he praised you in the midnight hour and then stepped out of the prison walls to continue in your service. You ordered King David's steps when he was a young boy to step up and defeat a giant with overwhelming size beyond his own.

Lord, order my steps in faith and prayer. I need your power all the days of my life. Help me that at the end, I may dwell in the house of the Lord all the days of my life. Lord, I need you right now in my life. And Father, not only do I pray for me, but I pray for your power of protection and deliverance to rest upon my fellow soldiers and all the commands of the armed forces of America, the Senate, the House of Representatives, the President's Cabinet, the Vice-President, and upon the Commander in Chief (President of the United States). I give you praise, Father, in Jesus's name, amen.

My Faith in God: My faith helps me order my steps, no matter where I am. In Jesus Christ.

Confess and believe!

Today I confess giving God all the glory, for He is the only true and wise God. Holy, holy, holy is the name of Jesus Christ. We must recognize His awesome goodness.

FAITH IS VICTORY IN GOD

Whatever is born of God overcomes the world. And this is the victory that has overcome the world—our faith. (1 John 5:4)

One might be the President of the United States or the highest ranking general, a field-grade officer or junior officer, a command sergeant major (CSM/SGM) or a first sergeant (1SG), a platoon sergeant or squad leader or anyone enlisted in the armed forces—whatever the rank structure might be in any branch of service, God wants you to know that your faith in Him counts, and He loves you with an everlasting love. He wants to come into your heart. He wants you to know that He will help you if you trust Him.

Father, I thank you for encouraging me to have faith that overcomes the world and everything that challenges me. Your word says that whatever is born of God overcomes the world. And this is the victory, that I have overcome the world through faith. Lord, please never allow me to lose sight of the fact that I am born again and have committed my life to Jesus Christ as my personal Savior. Help me, Lord, to know the power of faith that gives victory.

You gave me faith to help me overcome my struggles and my difficulties of life. Help me overcome the difficulties of alcoholism and drug addiction. Lord, help me defeat the enemy in my house. I claim victory today. Help me overcome the enemy every time he approaches to entice or tempt me with sin. I will confess my victory in Christ Jesus who has the delivered me from the world's view of victory, fame, money, and high places to a spiritual view of victory in Jesus Christ. Keep me humble and obedient to walk in victory by faith, Lord. Keep my heart on you and your eternal love. In Christ Jesus.

My Faith in God: My faith in the Lord Jesus Christ helps me overcome every obstacle.

Confess and believe!

Today, I confess that Jesus is Lord of my life and I will walk in victory especially when times get hard.

VICTORY OVER DEATH

So when this corruptible has put on incorruption, and this mortal has put on immortality, then shall be brought to pass the saying that is written: "Death is swallowed up in victory." (1 Corinthians 15:54)

Lord, thank you for victory over death. Your precious blood washed my sin away. Your precious blood is the reason why all your saints have the victory in Jesus Christ. Your love and kindness make me victorious. You always bless me and give new and tender mercies each day in my life. Thank you for defeating the enemy and the sting of death. You are God all by yourself and worthy of all praise, exaltation, and worship throughout all eternity. I bow down before you Lord, day and night. My heart belongs to you.

Thank you for your plan to change me in a twinkling of an eye in the Spirit. Because of you, I live in this body of corruptible flesh; however, you have fixed it so I will put on incorruption. You fixed it so I can put on immortality. My life will be real with you in spirit and truth forever upon your return. Lord you are the reason why I can walk in the Spirit and expect the abundance of life and victory in Jesus Christ.

My Faith in God: My faith helps me know that I have the victory over the sting of death and all things that trouble me. Jesus Christ is the giver of this victory!

Confess and believe!

Today I confess giving God all the glory, for He is the one who stirs my heart and keeps my life on track and walking in victory.

BE WATCHFUL

But you be watchful in all things, endure afflictions, do the work of an evangelist, fulfill your ministry. (2 Timothy 4:5)

God wants those in the ministry to be watchful of things that interrupt, entangle, block, hurt, confuse, destroy, and portray ungodliness in life and in the ministry. Be watchful in all things, even those things not mentioned here. God wants us to evangelize in order to reach the world.

Father, help me be watchful of the things in my life. Help me keep my eyes on you, the solid rock of salvation. You said to be watchful in all things, endure afflictions, and do the work of an evangelist. I pray to be ready in season and out of season with the aid of your Holy Spirit. Because a time will come when those of the world will not hear the Lord's preaching, we must be watchful and ready to lead lost souls into the kingdom of God.

Lord, help me to be on the lookout post as a guard of the United States armed forces. Help me to be on lookout as a minister of the gospel. Help me to fulfill my ministry according to your purpose and give you all the glory.

My Faith in God: My faith helps me be watchful at all things that I need to be watchful for.

Confess and believe!

Today I confess that as the Holy Spirit guides me in Spirit and truth, I will be watchful that I act in obedience.

WAVERING

Let us hold fast the confession of our hope without wavering, for He who promised is faithful. (Hebrews 10:23)

You waver when you are indecisive, when you cannot make up your mind. Wavering refers to those who go back and forth, who are not stable, especially in the ministry. Wavering is like a ship tossed to and fro in the waters under a raging wind. Typically, these are people who do not have their minds made up. These are people who do not have an anchor. They are not rooted or grounded in Jesus Christ. They lack faith. Jesus is reaching out every day to strengthen people in faith and love under the power of the Holy Spirit. No more playing around. God wants people to stop pretending to love Him. Start today opening your heart fully for Jesus to come in. Turn your life around and serve God, not money, nor any other thing. Say this prayer:

Father, I pray to have a hold-fast spirit. I desire to be a doer of the faith and not waver. Lord, you are faithful and you never waver. Help me be like you, Jesus. Thank you for revealing my ways to me. Thank you for encouraging me to become faithful. Regardless of the weight and pain and agonies in my life, I acknowledge you today as Lord of my life.

Lord, you set the example by showing us real action and not wavering. You fed over 500 people with a few fish and bread. You hit the ground running when God, your Father. placed you on earth. You did not think twice about serving our Father in heaven. You showed your power through miracles at the wedding in Cana in Galilee where you turned water into wine. You also cleansed lepers and raised the dead, when no one else would touch them. You set the stage for every Christian to witness and testify of your goodness. I will witness and testify of you to everyone I know. You personally blessed me. I will tell them that you died and rose from the dead so that I could have eternal life. I will bless the Lord at all times. His praise shall continually be in my mouth.

My Faith in God: My faith helps me stop wavering and procrastinating but instead be about my Father's business.

Confess and believe!

Today I confess that I will not waver anymore in my life. The Lord has change my mind to think positive and walk with confident and faith.

WORRY

Therefore I say to you, do not worry about your life, what you will eat or what you will drink; nor about your body, what you will put on. Is not life more than food and the body more than clothing? (Matthew 6:25)

Lord, you teach us that you will provide for us. You already know the plan for my life and for everyone in the world. Teach us to focus on you and have faith that you will provide.

I pray for a new focus in life. Lord, help me get over my worries and my doubts. You have already proved yourself by dying on the cross and rising from the dead. There is no reason for me to walk around worrying knowing that my Master has all power in His hand. You even reminded us that the birds of the air are already provided for. If you can provide for birds, you definitely know my needs and can provide according to your will.

Keep me from the worrying state of mind. Help me not to worry about my family at home while I fight this war in Iraq and Afghanistan. Keep my faith strong in your will and provisions for my life.

My Faith in God: My faith helps me stop worrying about everything. I will give it to the Lord Jesus Christ.

Confess and believe!

Today I confess giving God all the glory because He helps me through those times of worrying about things I should not worry about. He keeps my mind stable when things try to distract me.

WAITING ON THE LORD

But those who wait on the Lord shall renew their strength; they shall mount up with wings like eagles, they shall run and not be weary, they shall walk and not faint. (Isaiah 40:31)

Almighty God, your word says those who wait on the Lord shall renew their strength; they shall mount up with wings like eagles, they shall run and not be weary, they shall walk and not faint. You made that eagle to have focused power and strength in the air. You even gave him special abilities to see.

Lord, help me when the weariness of life interferes in my serving for you. Help me when things interfere to destroy me, my family, and my friends. Supply me with the endurance to withstand those weak and weary moments. Walk with me through trials that hurt and test me. Strengthen me in patience, and refresh me at home, at work, and during combat operations. Help my combat buddies to be vigorous in their dealing in military affairs. Help all my friends in combat and at home to accept you as Lord in their hearts today!

My Faith in God: My faith helps me wait on God. He must have a blessing waiting to pour out in my life.

Confess and believe!

Today I confess that I will wait on the Lord and not be hasty for anything. Lord give me patience to wait on you for my ministry, my marriage and all the blessings that you have for me.

LAUGHTER AND WEEPING

[There is] a time to weep, and a time to laugh.
(Ecclesiastes 3:4)

Lord, thank you for knowing all about time. You set the time in motion for each person's life. When seasons come and go, you already know when it will happen. During changing times, you remain the same God yesterday, today, and forevermore.

Father, you said that there is a time for everything. You said, there is a time to weep, a time to laugh; and a time to mourn. Lord, there is a time you gave us to comfort each other when weeping comes upon us. You gave a time to laugh at something that brings us together. It could be as funny as watching a comedy show or a 3-D cartoon. You helped me laugh at the movie called *Home Alone*. I laughed so much that I had to watch it again. Continue to help me laugh and not be too serious.

Lord also uphold me and wipe my tears away with your love and kindness that I might smile again and laugh again after my weeping period is over. You said in your word, that "weeping may endure for a night, but joy comes in the morning" (Psalm 30:5). In Jesus's name, amen.

My Faith in God: My faith deals with the time to weep, laugh, and rejoice when God puts it on my heart. He already knows the time and place and why.

Confess and believe!

Today I confess that my time belongs to you. I pray to give you more time of my life in service and worship. You have blessed me with time to take care daily business. If it were not for you, I would not have anytime. Praise to your Holy name.

WORSHIP GOD ALONE

The hour is coming, and now is, when the true worshipers will worship the Father in spirit and truth; for the Father is seeking such to worship Him. God is Spirit, and those who worship Him must worship in spirit and truth. (John 4:23-24)

Lord, help us remember that you gave us an example of true worshipers. You said God is a Spirit and those who worship Him must worship him in spirit and truth. Father, help me worship you everywhere I go in spirit and truth. Help me focus on you in worship. I pray to remain focused in my worship life. Lord, I exalt your name. Lord, I will continue to worship you because my life has changed. I will worship you as long as I live.

My Faith in God: My faith helps me worship God in spirit and truth. It is a blessing and life changing when I worship my Lord Jesus Christ. Don't let anything stop you.

Confess and believe!

Today, I confess that my worship life in Jesus Christ has blessed me and keeps my mind and spirit connected to Him.

THE WORD OF GOD

For the word of God is quick, and powerful, and sharper than any twoedged sword, piercing even to the dividing asunder of soul and spirit, and of the joints and marrow, and is a discerner of the thoughts and intents of the heart. (Hebrews 4:12 KJV)

Your word is a lamp to my feet and a light to my path. (Psalm 119:105)

Lord, your word has all power in it. You tell us that the word is quick, powerful, and sharper than any two-edged sword. I am convinced that your word can do anything. Thank you for assuring me through David that your word is a lamp to my feet and a light to my path. Lord Jehovah, your word guides me through the highways, the hills and mountains of my life. Lord, provide light for the dark places that I may travel along. Lead me in the paths of righteousness for your name's sake. Lord, you said that the grass withers, the flowers fade, but the word of our God stands forever. So I pray, Lord, as David did, that I will hide your word in my heart that I might not sin against you. Keep your light shining forever, in Jesus's name, amen.

My Faith in God: My faith takes me to the word of God for all things. I pray for obedience to search the scriptures for life.

Confess and believe!

Today I confess that God's word has penetrated my heart and made me believe in His awesome power and love.

WISDOM

PROVERBS 4:5 Get wisdom! Get understanding! Do not forget, nor turn away from the words of my mouth. (Proverbs 4:5)

King Solomon was known to be the wisest man in the world. He was wise because he asked God for wisdom. Father, you command us to get wisdom and understanding. You said not to forget or turn away from the words of your mouth. Lord, as a man and a soldier of the armed forces, help me have wisdom and knowledge in my duties and at home. Lord, you said happy is the man who finds wisdom and the man who gains understanding. Lord, I pray to walk in wisdom.

My Faith in God: My faith helps me walk with wisdom as I count on you, Lord Jesus.

Confess and believe!

Today I confess giving God all the glory because His wisdom exceeds all of mankind. He always direct me on the right path of life.

Winning Souls

The fruit of the righteous is a tree of life; and he that winneth souls is wise. (Proverbs 11:30 KJV)

Almighty God, help me have a winning spirit on the battlefield, as I serve the military, and more importantly, at home with my family. However, nothing prepares me like winning souls for God's Army. Lord, thank you for showing that winning souls matters to you. Help me be patient in all that I do, especially with my family and my team of soldiers. Lord, thank you for not allowing defeat to drift into my mind. I rebuke any thoughts of defeat and anything less than winning in your kingdom, and on this battlefield. I will remain encouraged through the battle and storm. I thank you for encouragement to be the best that I can be. I pray to be righteous in your Spirit, so that fruit may come forth because of your loving kindness. I pray to win souls even in the worst of conditions on the battlefield and elsewhere. Thank you for allowing me to accept you as Lord and Savior in my life. Because you came into my heart, I am now on the winning side. Lord, guide me to win souls for your kingdom and that they will surrender their wills to you and exalt your name. In Jesus's name, amen.

My Faith in God: My faith in God is what helps me win souls for Jesus Christ.

Confess and believe!

Today, I confess giving God all the glory as I go out to tell someone of His love and power in my life. I know souls need to be saved. I will tell them to stop rejecting God in their life.

HEALING WOUNDS

But He was wounded for our transgressions, He was bruised for our iniquities: the chastisement of our peace was upon him; and with his stripes we are healed. (Isaiah 53:5 KJV)

When was the last time someone got wounded for you? As soldiers you are on the battlefield, you stand guard to protect innocent people, yet Jesus was sent to show a love like no other to all people.

Father, you blessed me and the entire world with your Son, Jesus Christ. Jesus took my wounds away and placed them on His body. He took upon Himself all my troubles and my disobedient way of life. Thank you not only that you set me free but that the world was set free by the power of your love. My transgressions are dismissed because of your love, Lord. Thank you, Father! You decided to send Jesus as the ultimate sacrifice who took my pain and agony. In Jesus's name, amen.

My Faith in God: My faith helps me seek God for healing in Jesus Christ's name.

Confess and believe!

Today I confess giving God all the glory, for He is the only true and wise God. Holy, holy, holy is the name of Jesus Christ. We must recognize His awesome goodness.

JESUS CARES MORE THAN ANYONE

Casting all your care upon him; for he careth for you. (1 Peter 5:7)

Caring for other people is something special from God. But the ultimate person who will always take care of me is the Lord. I can give Him all my cares today, and He will see me through.

Lord, you said to cast my care upon you, for you care. Help me cast my cares about things in this present world. Help me deal with the things of war in Iraq and those experiences in Afghanistan. Help me deal with the people I love and other members of my family and those I am associated with. You are able to see all things and hear all things, and there is nothing hid from you. Even the things I think of, you already know about them. You have already made plans in my life to take care of all my concerns and problems. Your mercy and grace sustain us. In our Lord's name, amen.

My Faith in God: My faith helps me care for people.

Confess and believe!

Today I confess giving God all the glory, because I can cast my cares on Him. My care get heavy in my life but when I give them to Jesus, my life is turned around. Praise and glory to Jesus Christ.

TRUST IN THE LORD

Trust in the Lord with all thine heart; and lean not unto thine own understanding. In all thy ways acknowledge him, and he shall direct thy path. Proverbs 3:5-6 (KJV)

Father, you said to trust you with all my heart and lean not to my own understanding; in all my ways I am to acknowledge you, and you will direct my paths. Lord, serving in war and training exercises made me realize that I need someone I can trust and depend on daily. Lord, I trust you to keep me safe and on the right path of life. Help me to stay off the path of destruction that leads to self-destruction. I pray to fully trust you, Lord.

My Faith in God helps me trust Him to overcome my enemies. When prey such as demons of lust attack and try taking control of me, God always see me through.

Confess and believe!

Today I confess giving God all the glory because I can trust Him. I know that God will never fail. He never gives up on me.

JUDGE NOT

Judge not, that you be not judged. For with what judgment you judge, you will be judged. (Matthew 7:1-2)

Father, help me not to judge and criticize others. Help me lift people up when they feel put down. Strengthen me to encourage others instead of having an evil spirit that negatively judges others. Only you can help me improve in those areas of life that need help. When others are weak, bless me to bless others when they need help in life. Allow us to correct each other with love when needed. However, remove the hypocrisy from my eye and from others, so we can see clearly. Lord, you remind us to treat people with kindness and not judge harshly. Lord, give me the right things to say to family, friends, and the people I meet. Help me do everything in love and kindness. In Jesus's name.

> **My Faith in God: My faith helps me seek God and not judge people wrongly. However, do everything in love and kindness.**

Confess and believe!

Today I confess giving God all the glory because He is the true judge. No one can escape Him. God sees all things good and bad. He knows every situation in everyone's life.

SEEKING GOD

Seek, and you will find; knock, and it will be opened to you.
(Matthew 7:7)

Lord, I have sought after many things in my life and ended up with many disappointments. Many of those disappointments were huge and overwhelming, with great weights. Now that my eyes and my spirit are open to you, I can believe again and trust in you alone. I am now aware that I must "seek first the kingdom of God and His righteousness," and everything else will follow, according to Matthew 6:33.

Father, you have all the answers for my life. You hold my life in the palm of your hand. I thank you for placing me on the right path of life in your kingdom with a destination to heaven when you return. Now my hope is to be pleasing in your sight. Lord, you said, "Seek and you shall find." I will seek you in all things in my life from this day on. In my daily meditation I will seek you for answers and guidance. When heartaches and disappointments arise, I will seek you for comfort and resolution. When trouble is on every side and seems to exhaust my spirit man, I will seek you because I know with all my heart that I can depend on your hedge of protection and on strength from you.

For the rest of my life my heart will seek you. Thank you for giving me a life predestined under your authority and will. Therefore, my prayer is always to strive for humility, obedience, and commitment to you as a servant in your kingdom. I pray to seek you in all things, even in my weakest hour, and in all challenges. Lord, I will seek you in the morning, at noon, and even in the midnight hour. As I seek you, I know that doors will open. And I know that when you open doors, no man can shut them. I am blessed with multiple blessings that come from you, my Lord Jesus. All praise to your Holy name.

My Faith in God: My faith helps me find my brother and sister.

Confess and believe!

Today I confess giving God all the glory, for He is the only true and wise God. Holy, holy, holy is the name of Jesus Christ. We must recognize His awesome goodness.

WALK IN THE SPIRIT

If we live in the Spirit, let us walk in the Spirit. Let us not become conceited, provoking one another, envying one another. (Galatians 5:25-26)

Lord, help me live and walk in the Spirit. I desire to walk in the Spirit so that my service in your kingdom will be pleasing in your sight. Help me avoid the old man and become the new man in Jesus Christ. Help me by the power of your Holy Spirit to reflect your image. I want to make you proud of me, Lord. Use me for your purpose and glory. I used to walk one way while I was in the world. I walked as a sinner, in love with doing things displeasing to God. I used to do things in the military that were not pleasing in God's sight. Today, help me, Lord, to change my walk permanently, so that I will tell the world of your grace, mercy, and loving kindness. Help me reflect godliness to my family and everyone I come in contact with. In Jesus's name, amen.

My Faith in God: My faith helps me walk in the Spirit.

Confess and believe!

Today I confess giving God all the glory, for He is the only true and wise God. Holy, holy, holy is the name of Jesus Christ. We must recognize His awesome goodness.

WORRY

Be careful for nothing; but in every thing by prayer and supplication with thanksgiving let your requests be made known unto God. And the peace of God, which passeth all understanding, shall keep your hearts and minds through Christ Jesus. (Philippians 4:6-7 KJV)

Lord, help me not to worry about things I have no control over, the things I am unable to restore or resolve. Allow me to depend solely on you through prayers of faith. Lord, you said that you are my hiding place; you shall preserve me from trouble; you shall compass me about with songs of deliverance. Selah. Lord, place my confidence in you and your will.

My Faith in God: My faith helps me trust God and stop worrying about things that only He can fix.

Confess and believe!

Today I confess giving God all the glory, for He is the only true and wise God. Holy, holy, holy is the name of Jesus Christ. We must recognize His awesome goodness.

REST

Come to Me, all you who labor and are heavy laden, and I will give you rest. Take My yoke upon you and learn from Me, for I am gentle and lowly in heart, and you will find rest for your souls. For My yoke is easy and My burden is light. (Matthew 11:28-30)

Lord, I am a soldier with many heavy burdens, and I surrender for you to lift them. War is my burden; my friend's death is a burden. You said, "Come to Me, all who labor and are heavy laden, and I will give you rest. Take My yoke upon you and learn from Me, for I am gentle and lowly in heart, and you will find rest for your souls. For My yoke is easy and my burden is light." Lord, remove the past abuse, rape, depression, and addictions. Lord I pray that you lift the guilt that will change somebody's life. Lift this guilt feels so heavy. Lord, you said to lay aside every weight that so easily besets me. Lord, only you can lift burdens and take over the struggles in my life. Only you can give rest to a weary soul like mine. Lord, rescue me and give me rest.

My Faith in God: My faith helps me rest in my Lord Jesus Christ.

Confess and believe!

Today I confess giving God the glory because He has given me rest for my soul.

FORGIVENESS

And whenever you stand praying, if you have anything against anyone, forgive him, that your Father in heaven may also forgive you your trespasses. (Mark 11:25)

Forgiveness is the most powerful thing you can do. Jesus forgave everybody. What does forgiveness mean? It means getting over the hurt and pain caused by someone else. It means not living with hatred in your heart. It means loving someone even when they hurt you. Forgiveness means not harboring anything that causes division.

Father, thank you for forgiving me for my sin against you. Help me follow your example of forgiveness, especially when my temper explodes and I go out of control. You said, "When you stand praying, if you hold anything against anyone, forgive him, so that your Father in heaven may forgive you your sins." In the midst of the deployment to Iraq and having mission challenges of seeking and finding the enemy, somehow, Lord, I fail to forgive my team and my buddy for their trespasses.

My Faith in God: My faith helps me seek God and forgive others as He instructs me.

Confess and believe!

Today I confess giving God all the glory, for He is the only true and wise God. Holy, holy, holy is the name of Jesus Christ. We must recognize His awesome goodness.

HEROES OF FAITH

Now faith is the substance of things hoped for, the evidence of things not seen. For by it the elders obtained a good testimony. By faith we understand that the worlds were framed by the word of God, so that things which are seen were not made of things which are visible. (Hebrews 11:1-3)

Father, I thank you for revealing your power through creation and your men of faith. You show us men and women of faith in the Bible who counted on you to witness and spread the word of God. Thank you for the faith that you give me each day.

Help me walk in faith when I am challenged by predators. Help me be a mighty man of faith as if a lion was chasing one of your sheep. Lord, I know you would protect me. I count on your power as Elijah did when faced with Jezebel and her prophets. Lord, increase my faith where I am weak. I desire the kind of faith that the heroes of faith had.

I pray to follow Jesus's example of faith. I am praying that my faith is perfected in your Lord as servant. I pray for faith to understand your word and believe in you in all things. I pray to follow you. I am blessed to know that you framed the world with your words.

My Faith in God: My faith helps me seek God and hope to walk in faith.

Confess and believe!

Today I confess giving God all the glory, for He is the only true and wise God. Holy, holy, holy is the name of Jesus Christ. We must recognize His awesome goodness.

MY TEENAGERS
OVERCOME FEAR

***For God has not given us a spirit of fear, but of power and
of love and of a sound mind. (2 Timothy 1:7)***

Lord, thank you for giving me a spirit of power, love, and a disciplined
mind. Help my teenagers trust in you, so that each one will overcome
their fears that keep them from receiving all the benefits and gifts for their
lives offered by you.

Father, even while I am deployed fighting a war for freedom, help my
teenagers overcome the fears of my duties in combat and their duties as
children. Remind them that you are the giver of power, the giver of love,
and the giver of a strong foundational mind. Strengthen them on a daily
basis while I am away and even upon my return. In you precious name,
Lord, Amen.

> **My Faith in God: My faith helps me seek God and
> helps teenagers overcome fears and other identity
> issues.**

Confess and believe!

Today I confess giving God all the glory, for He is the only true and wise
God. Holy, holy, holy is the name of Jesus Christ. We must recognize His
awesome goodness.

TEEN MIND-SET

And you, fathers, do not provoke your children to wrath, but bring them up in the training and admonition of the Lord. (Ephesians 6:4)

Lord, you spoke of children in the Bible when you said "train up a child in the way he should go." Father, I pray for my children as teenagers to reflect your image. You know how to handle the way of my children. Remind them that their body is the temple of God. I pray that in everything my children do, they reflect Jesus Christ in their walk.

My Faith in God: My faith helps me seek God to fill my thirst when I feel empty, lonely, confused or lost. I desire that you fill me with your love, Lord Jesus Christ.

Confess and believe!

Today I confess giving God all the glory, for He is the only true and wise God. Holy, holy, holy is the name of Jesus Christ. We must recognize His awesome goodness.

TEENS, GIVE IN TO GOD, NOT TROUBLE!

My son, if sinful men entice you, do not give in to them. (Proverbs 1:10 NIV)

Teenagers are precious in God's sight, just like all His children, Tell all the children in your house regardless of age to go to the Lord in prayer for every situation. Make sure you learn to thank God also.

Lord, I rely on your for strength when I am in trouble and hurt. Lord, help my children not to run with the wrong crowd, that brings negative influence. Place them with positive influences. Your word says you are my high tower and my shield. I will trust in you in all things. When you see me walking in the midst of enticement and bad influence, help me pull myself out of potential trouble. Help me to get out of the sin that lurks,

I thank you that you have protected my teenagers and my household completely. I ask, Lord, that you continue to watch over my family in times of need. Lord, keep them from activities and influences that might try to entice them and lead them astray. I am in the United States armed forces and deployed to a foreign land. My heart's desire is that my children are monitored and led by you, Lord. Help them by the power of your Holy Spirit to study your word, be obedient to my wife, and associate with those of positive influence while still enabled to help those in need. In your precious name, amen.

My Faith in God: My faith helps me help teens to pull themselves out of trouble.

Confess and believe!

Today I confess giving God all the glory, for He is the only true and wise God. Holy, holy, holy is the name of Jesus Christ. We must recognize His awesome goodness.

TEAMWORK

Now I am no longer in the world, but these are in the world, and I come to You. Holy Father, keep through Your name those whom You have given Me, that they may be one as We are. (John 17:11)

Lord, teach me to be better with my team when we go on missions and when we perform as a team. Jesus said, "Father, keep through your name those whom You have given me, that they may be one as We are." Lord, help my team when we face challenges as though we were on an obstacle course. Help my team survive on this battlefield with its dangerous obstacles. Never allow me to concentrate on being the first place winner, but help me function and finish the course as a team, just as Jesus did through His ministry and at the cross. Thank you that Jesus poured His heart out to His disciples in that He was never alone. He always remembered his team of disciples.

My Faith in God: My faith helps me seek God to be a better team member at home and at work.

Confess and believe!

Today I confess giving God all the glory, for He is the only true and wise God. Holy, holy, holy is the name of Jesus Christ. We must recognize His awesome goodness.

GOVERNMENT AUTHORITY

*Let every soul be subject to the governing authorities. For
there is no authority except from God, and the authorities
that exist are appointed by God. (Romans 13:1)*

Father, help me be obedient under the authority of those that you have
appointed over me. Help me and my leaders as we watch over many
communities and neighborhoods only under your power of protection.
Keep us from nuclear weapons and other weapons of mass destruction
which could result in mass casualties by terrorists.

Lord, I pray you continue to give your angels charge to deter terrorism
from this nation and other nations as well. Help our government leaders
to focus their efforts on our primary needs of security and welfare through
this country and neighboring countries. Help economies all around the
world. Help countries that are struggling with medical concerns. Send
your angels to help countries such as Haiti, Africa, India and others all
over the world that are affect by floods and natural disasters. In Jesus's
name, amen.

**My Faith in God: My faith helps me be subject to the
governing authorities.**

Confess and believe!

Today I confess giving God all the glory because you have all authority
over Presidents, Kings, Prince and all those in authority. You have blessed
governments and expect them to glorify you.

YOU HAVE BENEFITS

Bless the Lord, O my soul; and all that is within me, bless His holy name! Bless the Lord, O my soul, and forget not all His benefits: who forgives all your iniquities, who heals all your diseases, who redeems your life from destruction. (Psalm 103:1-4)

You have unlimited benefits if you are in Jesus Christ. Blessings are laid up for you.

Lord, thank you for allowing me to be healthy for so many years especially those in the armed forces. You kept me in excellent condition then. Keep me now, Lord. You said that you heal all diseases. You proved that to me by healing lepers, blind men, lame men, a woman with a blood issue, a paralyzed man, and all manner of sickness. Your hold all power in the palm of your hand. No one is like you, Sovereign God. I thank you for the benefits that you are able to deliver to us as believers. I ask that you heal me from all my conditions. If it is heart disease, heal me. Lord, heal my family and friends from cancer, AIDS, drug addiction, and all sicknesses that create handicaps, crippling conditions, and suffering. Restore me to a healthy condition that I might serve you wholeheartedly. In Jesus's name, amen.

My Faith in God: My faith helps me know I have benefits laid up in the form of blessings.

Confess and believe!

Today I confess giving God all the glory because of the benefits you give me in life. I would not own anything if it were not for you. You keep blessings flowing in my life.

RESURRECTION

If we have been united together in the likeness of His death, certainly we also shall be in the likeness of His resurrection, knowing this, that our old man was crucified with Him, that the body of sin might be done away with, that we should no longer be slaves of sin. (Romans 6:5-6)

Almighty God, you allowed me to personally experience the power of your resurrection in my life. You said, "If we have been united together in the likeness of His death, certainly we also shall be in the likeness of His resurrection." Help me with my desire to walk in the power of your resurrection. Give me the words to express it to my family, fellow soldiers, friends, and anyone I come into contact with throughout the world.

Your word says, "that I may know Him and the power of His resurrection, and the fellowship of His sufferings, being conformed to His death." Help me always know you, Lord, now and throughout eternity. Thank you because it is your blood that covers the multitude of sins. It was your blood and the power of your resurrection that removed and destroyed sin once and for all. You took the sting of death from me and everyone else. I thank you, Lord, for your blessings of love.

My Faith in God: My faith helps me seek God to be a better team member at home and at work.

Confess and believe!

Today I confess giving God all the glory, for He is the only true and wise God. Holy, holy, holy is the name of Jesus Christ. We must recognize His awesome goodness.

THE SABBATH

For the Son of Man is Lord even of the Sabbath.
(Matthew 12:8)

Father, help me honor and recognize the Sabbath. Lord, you set the Sabbath day aside for men to worship and to rest. You said, "Remember the Sabbath and keep it holy." You gave us the seventh day to rest and worship you according to the book of Genesis.

Lord, you said that the Son of Man is Lord even of the Sabbath. Lord, you gave us an example when you said, "What man is there among you who has one sheep, and if it falls into a pit on the Sabbath, will not lay hold of it and lift it out?" (Matthew 12:11). Lord, give me a heart to help others when I run across them on any day, including the Sabbath. God is looking at the heart of man to love your neighbor rather worry about the Sabbath day.

Thank you for sacrificing your life on Calvary that I could be lifted from the pits of sin. You saved me because of your love. You did not wait; you just saved me. Help me make every day of my life an expression of the Sabbath in worship and service as I help those in need.

God wants us to do real ministry instead of getting confused about blessing others. Thank you for blessing the Sabbath and hallowing it. Lord, wherever I go, may I express thankfulness to you for the Sabbath while serving you in the armed forces, even in time of war. In your precious name, Jesus Christ, amen.

My Faith in God: My faith helps me seek God to be a better man at home and at work.

Confess and believe!

Today I confess giving God all the glory, for He is the only true and wise God. Holy, holy, holy is the name of Jesus Christ. We must recognize His awesome goodness.

PUT ON GOD'S LOVE

Therefore, as the elect of God, holy and beloved, put on tender mercies, kindness, humility, meekness, longsuffering; bearing with one another, and forgiving one another, if anyone has a complaint against another; even as Christ forgave you, so you also must do. But above all these things put on love, which is the bond of perfection. And let the peace of God rule in your hearts, to which also you were called in one body, and be thankful. (Colossians 3:12-15)

Lord, thank you for the power of love. God is love The very meaning of love comes from you. You clothe us in love by your blessed power. You love is better than life itself. Your love is better than wine. Your love is better than all things. Your love never fails me. Your love is deeper than the deepest ocean.

Thank you for showing me the way even while I was in combat in Iraq, even while I was in combat in Afghanistan. Lord, you have been so kind and gentle to me. You have even shown me the way at home. Help me this day, Father, to put on love in such a way that my heart will be clothed forever and pleasing in your sight. Thank you for being the one who fills my heart with your love.

I know that I can only put on tender mercies, kindness, humility, meekness, longsuffering, love, and the spirit of forgiveness by your Holy Spirit's power. I pray that, after this war or even before the end, I may put on the bond of perfection which is the love that God always gives to us. I pray that the peace of God rules in my heart, mind, soul, and spirit. Today is the day that I change my life. Father, it was your protection that kept me and saw me through the storms of battles and all the firepower around my head. I know this day that I could have easily been broken and easily became a casualty of war for the rest of my life. I thank you that wounds will heal because of your love for healing. So Lord, I praise you with the most powerful adoration. I glorify your righteous name. In Jesus's name, amen.

My Faith in God: My faith helps me put on the love of God at home and at work. This will help me help someone change from their ways.

Confess and believe!

Today I confess giving God all the glory, for He is the only true and wise God. Holy, holy, holy is the name of Jesus Christ. We must recognize His awesome goodness.

TEN COMMANDMENTS

And God spoke all these words, saying:

"I am the LORD your God, who brought you out of the land of Egypt, out of the house of bondage.

"You shall have no other gods before Me.

"You shall not make for yourself a carved image any likeness of anything that is in heaven above, or that is in the earth beneath, or that is in the water under the earth; you shall not bow down to them nor serve them. For I, the LORD your God, am a jealous God, visiting the iniquity of the fathers upon the children to the third and fourth generations of those who hate Me, but showing mercy to thousands, to those who love Me and keep My commandments.

"You shall not take the name of the LORD your God in vain, for the LORD will not hold him guiltless who takes His name in vain.

"Remember the Sabbath day, to keep it holy. Six days you shall labor and do all your work, but the seventh day is the Sabbath of the LORD your God. In it you shall do no work: you, nor your son, nor your daughter, nor your male servant, nor your female servant, nor your cattle, nor your stranger who is within your gates. For in six days the LORD made the heavens and the earth, the sea, and all that is in them, and rested the seventh day. Therefore the LORD blessed the Sabbath day and hallowed it.

"Honor your father and your mother, that your days may be long upon the land which the LORD your God is giving you.

"You shall not murder.

"You shall not commit adultery.

"You shall not steal.

"You shall not bear false witness against your neighbor.

"You shall not covet your neighbor's house; you shall not covet your neighbor's wife, nor his male servant, nor his female servant, nor his ox, nor his donkey, nor anything that is your neighbor's." (Exodus 20:1-17)

Lord, thank you for establishing the law on Mount Sinai. You led Moses to instruct your people because of the abundance of sin, the wickedness of their hearts. You gave us the Ten Commandments as a guide to live our lives after powerfully bringing your people out Egypt's bondage and sinful ways.

Your first law said we shall have no other god before you. Thank you, Lord, for removing idols that were formed to influence and invade my heart as lords of my life. Help me when temptation and evil attacks try to turn me in the direction of sin. I rebuke those sinful ways.

I cannot make it without you, Lord. Father, help me live by your standards of holiness, and turn me around when I am on the wrong path of life. In the blessed name of Jesus.

> **My Faith in God: My faith helps me seek God to fill my thirst when I feel empty, lonely, confused, or lost. I desire that you fill me with your love, Lord Jesus Christ.**

Confess and believe!

Today I confess giving God all the glory because you gave the ten commandments to help us to be obedient servants of God.

PRIDE

These six things the Lord hates,

Yes, seven are an abomination to Him:

A proud look,

A lying tongue,

Hands that shed innocent blood,

A heart that devises wicked plans,

Feet that are swift in running to evil,

A false witness who speaks lies,

And one who sows discord among brethren. (Proverbs 6:16-19)

Father, I need you to keep me from exhibiting those six prideful things that you mention in your word. Pride is just like something that could be a predator. If the seventh attacks us, I pray you instantly remove the spirit of discord among brethren. You always remind that pride comes before the fall. Keep me in your perfect will, Lord. Keep me humble before your throne of grace. In Jesus's name, amen.

My Faith in God: My faith helps me put off prideful things.

Confess and believe!

Today I confess giving God all the glory because He helps me get over my pride.

PATIENCE

Be kindly affectionate to one another with brotherly love, in honor giving preference to one another; not lagging in diligence, fervent in spirit, serving the Lord; rejoicing in hope, patient in tribulation, continuing steadfastly in prayer; distributing to the needs of the saints, given to hospitality. (Romans 12:10-13)

Lord, thank you for the patience you put inside my heart by your Holy Spirit. Keep patience in the forefront of my life as I pray and worship you. Also, keep me as I serve this military on deployment and upon return home. Help me be patient as I face this life and the challenges ahead.

Thank you for patience with other people in my life. Because of the patience you give me, I am able to make it through this war and the missions that I face. Because of the patience you give me, I am able to maintain a love for my family. Throughout the trials, upsets, and arrows that come my way, you make me a better person. In your precious name, amen.

My Faith in God: My faith helps me be patient with everyone at home and at work.

Confess and believe!

Today I honor God because he takes me by the hand and helps me to be a better person and patient with other people.

MANHOOD

***Then the Lord God formed a man from the dust of the
ground and breathed into his nostrils the breath of life, and
the man became a living being. (Genesis 2:7 NIV)***

The man was formed by God, and no one else can get credit. Manhood
was established when God formed him and breathed life into his nostrils.

Thank you, Jesus, for putting emphasis on the man. You made him to
be in your likeness. Thank you for making the man strong enough to be
connected to you, Lord. To complete the training process and cross over
into manhood, the man would have to become obedient to God. Father,
thank you for creating me as a man. Help me be pleasing in your sight as
I learn your Holy Word and walk by faith.

Lord, while I am deployed into Iraq, build me up to a better man. Help
me walk in the Spirit. Sometimes I feel that my manhood is challenged.
Lord, help me and my wife build a better marriage. Help her serve you
with all her heart. You have our future in your hands. Help me check my
manhood when I am not doing what is required of me as a man.

> **My Faith in God: My faith helps me walk in my
> manhood under the influence and power of the Holy
> Spirit at home, at work, and everywhere I go.**

Confess and believe!

Today I confess giving God all the glory because He helped me to become
a better man. He taught me the true meaning of manhood. He blessed me
to be transformed into a man of God.

A LIVING SACRIFICE

I beseech you therefore, brethren, by the mercies of God, that you present your bodies a living sacrifice, holy, acceptable to God, which is your reasonable service. (Romans 12:1)

Heavenly Father, your word through the Apostle Paul said, "I beseech you therefore, brethren, by the mercies of God, that you present your bodies a living sacrifice, holy, acceptable to God, which is your reasonable service." Since you desire me to present myself, today I surrender to you. I come before your altar presenting myself as a living sacrifice.

Lord, help me start by turning my heart, soul, and life over to you as a sacrifice. I have made many sacrifices as a soldier. My life was on the line many times on many deployments. Now I want to make sacrifice and put my life on the line with you, Lord.

Lord, accept me as a living sacrifice as you did your apostles, Paul, John, and James, that I may spread the gospel and tell of your greatness, goodness, and tender mercies. You said, "Do not be conformed to this world, but be transformed by the renewing of your mind, that you may prove what is that good and acceptable and perfect will of God" (Romans 12:2). Create in me a new mind by the power of the Holy Spirit. Allow me to serve to the best of my abilities in your kingdom by helping others. Also enable me to be a better witness to the soldiers that I work with now and those in the past. Guide me in making sacrifices that please you, Lord, while I serve the military and when I retire. In Jesus's name, amen.

My Faith in God: My faith helps me be a living sacrifice to God. I need to give God my reasonable service, since He always blesses me.

Confess and believe!

Today I confess giving God all the glory because He used Jesus as a sacrifice, Holy and acceptable in His sight. He used Jesus to help us live and serve as an example.

BE ENCOURAGED

I long to see you, that I may impart to you some spiritual gift, so that you may be established—that is, that I may encouraged together with you by the mutual faith both of you and me. (Romans 1:11-12)

Lord, Paul told the church in Rome that he desired much to impart some spiritual gifts among them in the church, so they would be established as a strong body of Christ. He stated that he wanted to be encouraged with the church by mutual faith.

Help me, Lord, to be encouraged in the areas where barriers exist. Help me worship you, serve you, praise you, and live a life holy and acceptable in your sight. Lord, I am a soldier and need your encouragement to be the best in my career while I also serve you.

My Faith in God: My faith encourages me on the tough days and times of letdown and enemy attacks.

Confess and believe!

Today I confess giving God all the glory because he encourages me to strive for excellence as I serve Him.

HAVE FAITH

And Jesus said unto them, Because of your unbelief: for verily I say unto you, If ye have faith as a grain of mustard seed, ye shall say unto this mountain, Remove hence to yonder place; and it shall remove; and nothing shall be impossible unto you. Matthew 17:20 (KJV)

Lord, help me have this kind of faith while I am a soldier in the armed forces. Help me be humble under the authority of those over me. Lord, you reminded me that with a mustard seed of faith things can change in my life. You tell us that mountains can be removed. Thank you for the encouragement to know that all those big issues can be moved by having faith in you Lord.

My Faith in God: I pray for faith that can move any kind of mountains in my life.

Confess and believe!

Today I confess giving God all the glory because He helps me walk in faith. Jesus always comes to my rescue because of my faith in Him.

ATTITUDE

And seeing the multitudes, He went up on a mountain, and when He was seated His disciples came to Him. Then He opened His mouth and taught them, saying:

"Blessed are the poor in spirit, for theirs is the kingdom of heaven.

Blessed are those who mourn, for they shall be comforted.

Blessed are the meek, for they shall inherit the earth.

Blessed are those who hunger and thirst for righteousness, for they shall be filled.

Blessed are the merciful, for they shall obtain mercy.

Blessed are the pure in heart, for they shall see God.

Blessed are the peacemakers, for they shall be called sons of God.

Blessed are those who are persecuted for righteousness' sake, for theirs is the kingdom of heaven." (Matthew 5:1-10)

Heavenly Father, your Son, Jesus, gave us the attitude we should live by. Jesus said, "Blessed are the poor in spirit, for theirs is the kingdom of heaven."

My Faith in God: My faith helps me put on the right attitude in every circumstance.

Confess and believe!

Today, I am determined to wait on God's move in my life. Whether it is today or tomorrow, I will walk in courage and in God's strength. All glory to your righteous name.

BLASPHEMY

Therefore I say to you, every sin and blasphemy will be forgiven men, but the blasphemy against the Spirit will not be forgiven men. (Matthew 12:31)

Saints and sinners, always live with the utmost reverence and honor for God. Give Him glory at all times. Thank Him, and never let a bad word come from your lips, especially using His name. He knows you by name, whatever you say and whatever you do. There is no hiding place from God. He knows where you are, so He can love you where you are.

Lord, forgive me when I fall short. Help me tell others that our lips were made to exalt you from our hearts and not use profane and babbling words against you or anyone else. I pray for the power of your Holy Spirit to teach me what I ought to say. Keep our words short and our focus on magnifying Jesus Christ. Lord, help me cautiously tell others not to use the Lord's name in vain.

> **My Faith in God: My faith helps me seek God to fill my thirst when I feel empty, lonely, confused, or lost. I desire that you fill me with your love, Lord Jesus Christ.**

Confess and believe!

Today I confess giving God all the glory because He forgives me of my sin.

GREAT FAITH

"I also am a man under authority, having soldiers under me. And I say to this one, 'Go,' and he goes; and to another, 'Come,' and he comes; and to my servant, 'Do this,' and he does it."

When Jesus heard it, He marveled, and said to those who followed, "Assuredly, I say to you, I have not found such great faith, not even in Israel!" (Matthew 8:9-10)

Father, thank you for recognizing my faith as a soldier serving my country and the people. Only you know the level of my faith. You know exactly where my heart and mind are with faith in you. Father, I pray to have great faith. Lord, help me have faith like the centurion soldier, who knew that, if you just spoke a word, his servant would be healed. Lord, no one is like you. No one can deliver people out of crisis and even when death is approaching. Father, you have a way about blessing us.

My Faith in God: My faith helps me to become a better leader in the military and on my job.

Confess and believe!

Today I confess giving God all the glory because he molded me into a better Soldier.

SELF-ESTEEM

> *. . . that the genuineness of your faith, being much more precious than gold that perishes, though it is tested by fire, may be found to praise, honor, and glory at the revelation of Jesus Christ, whom having not seen you love. Though now you do not see Him, yet believing, you rejoice with joy inexpressible and full of glory, receiving the end of your faith—the salvation of your souls. (1 Peter 1:7-9)*

Father, help me when I am feeling low. Help me cast my cares upon you. When I have difficulty with my depression and identity, help me get back on track. Help me have a firm grip on my identity.

Jesus asked Peter, during the establishment of the church, "Who do men say that I am?"

Peter said, "Some say Elijah, some say a prophet."

Jesus asked Peter, "Who do you say that I am?"

Peter said, "Thou art the Christ, the Son of the living God."

Jesus said, "Flesh and blood could not have revealed this to you, but my Father in heaven." (See Matthew 16:13-17.)

Lord, I ask you to give me the same spirit, that I might know you and know myself, that my mind will never sink low again. Reveal to me who I am in Christ Jesus. For you are my strength.

My Faith in God: My faith helps me to call on His name in times of trouble. He knows all about me and nothing can be hid.

Confess and believe!

Today I confess that Jesus is the Son of God. He comes from heaven and his power is everlasting. He is Holy and there is no one like Him.

SEEK GOD FIRST

But seek first the kingdom of God and His righteousness,
and all these things shall be added to you. (Matthew 6:33)

Father, your word says we are to seek first the kingdom of God and His righteousness, and all these things shall be added to us. Lord, as I press toward goals that I have made more important than you, guide me by your Holy Spirit to refocus my life to seek you first. Help me with my addiction of sex and alcohol as my images of worship. You said, "Seek and you will find, knock and the door shall be opened, ask and you shall receive." Lord, I am asking to not be self-seeking because it leads to sin but rather to seek you in spirit, that I might please you and glorify you.

My Faith in God: My faith helps me seek God in all things.

Confess and believe!

Today I confess giving God all the glory, for He is the only true and wise God. Holy, holy, holy is the name of Jesus Christ. We must recognize His awesome goodness.

SEEK GOD FOR EVERYTHING

*But seek first the kingdom of God and His righteousness,
and all these things shall be added to you. (Matthew 6:33)*

Father, you know my mind and heart. When I feel sickness or fear or anything attacks me, I will seek you, Lord.

I will keep my mind on seeking the kingdom of God and His righteousness. I know that He will give me an answer.

When I see a friend or a buddy facing suicidal thoughts, depression, loneliness, stigma, or any challenges mentally or physically, I pray, Lord, that you send your angels to help overcome any demons that prey against my life, family and friends. I also need your Holy Spirit to guide me in decisions to serve you. I pray for everyone in my entire family. I will seek you now and forever because of your loving kindness.

My Faith in God: My faith helps me put on the love of God at home and at work.

Confess and believe!

Today I confess giving God all the glory because only you Lord can give me strength to seek you and do the things that I can do on a daily basis.

A FAITHFUL SERVANT

His lord said to him, "Well done, good and faithful servant; you were faithful over a few things, I will make you rules over many things, Enter into the joy of your lord." (Matthew 25:21)

Lord, you inspired me to use my time, abilities, and wealth to serve you. You said, "Well done, good and faithful servant," to those who wisely invested the talents you gave them. Lead me to use all of my time, abilities, and wealth to uplift your kingdom. Allow me to dance with praise, sing and rejoice, do the work of an evangelist, and serve the poor and brokenhearted. Help me to enjoy through faithfulness what I perform for your service. I desire to be faithful in serving you.

Lord, you spoke to your servants and said, "You were faithful over a few things. I will make you ruler over many things. Enter into the joy of the lord." And Matthew 25:31 says, When the Son of Man comes in His glory, and all the holy angels with Him, then He will sit on the throne of His glory.

My Faith in God: My faith helps me put on the love of God at home and at work.

Confess and believe!

Today I confess giving God all the glory because is molding me and shaping my life to become a faithful servant.

SHEPHERD

I am the good shepherd. The good shepherd gives His life for the sheep. (John 10:11)

Lord, I thank you for being the Good Shepherd. I praise you because of your tender care. I thank you that you are able to lead me in every area of my life. Lord, continue to guide my life on the right path by your Holy Spirit. You encouraged David in his desperate time during leadership and companionship. You reminded David that he needed a Shepherd in his life to guide him.

As a soldier I need you with me on the battle field. You said, "I will fear no evil, for you are with me. Your rod and staff, they comfort me." Keep me through the battle and the scars and the wounds that will try to come against me. You said that the thief does not come except to steal, kill, and destroy. You said that you come to give life and that we may have it more abundantly. To the praise of your holy and righteous name.

My Faith in God: My faith helps me trust my Shepherd, Jesus Christ. He is my guide according to Psalm 23.

Confess and believe!

Lord, I give you praise because you are my Shepherd. You guard my life even when I do not deserve it.

ACKNOWLEDGE YOUR SIN

For I acknowledge my transgressions, and my sin is always before me. Against You, You only, have I sinned. (Psalm 51:3-4)

Lord, thank you for helping me recognize my sin and confess it before you. Lord, I sinned against you and need you to restore me. I realize that all power is in your hand, and you know what to do for my life. You know where I fall short in sin. Thank you for mercy.

My Faith in God: My faith helps me seek God and come before His presence with thanksgiving.

Confess and believe!

Today I confess giving God all the glory because he helped me to acknowledge my sin.

LORD, STRENGTHEN ME

The Lord is my light and my salvation; whom shall I fear?
The Lord is the strength of my life; of whom shall I be afraid?
(Psalm 27:1)

Lord, through the rough times of our missions, you are there. When I lost friends and had injuries in my unit, you managed to come and lift us up in your strength. You always show your loving kindness to your soldiers, even at moments in our lives that seem to be the worst. You strengthen me on patrol missions and through improvised explosive devices, booby-trapped, that could have taken my life. You are the God who really lives forever, and you have all power in your hand. Because of your loving kindness and your strength, I became stronger under your power. You are worthy of all praise, glory, and honor. Give me the strength to praise you. In the name of Jesus, amen.

My Faith in God: My faith helps me put on the love of God at home and at work.

Confess and believe!

Today I confess giving God all the glory because he has given me a heart to love right under the Holy Spirit.

STRIPPED!

We know that the law is spiritual, but I am carnal, sold under sin. For what I am doing, I do not understand. For what I will to do, that I do not practice; but what I hate, that I do. If, then, I do what I will not to do, I agree with the law that it is good. But now, it is no longer I who do it, but sin that dwells in me. For I know that in me (that is, in my flesh) nothing good dwells; for to will is present with me, but how to perform what is good I do not find. For the good that I will to do, I do not do; but the evil I will not to do, that I practice. Now if I do what I will not to do, it is no longer I who do it, but sin that dwells in me. (Romans 7:14-20)

Lord, thank you for revealing to me that nothing good dwells in me except Jesus Christ. I need you to help me do right in your eyes. Thank you for coming into my life when I felt like my dignity and pride were stripped from me. Thank you for comforting me even when I felt like my manhood had been stripped. Lord, thank you because you are always in my life to rescue me even when sin tries to take over my life. Thank you for being in the combat zone the days and nights I felt challenged and lonely. Thank you for being there when I needed someone to talk to. When my mind starts thinking that this war will never end, you manage to change my thinking and lift me up far from those thoughts. I thank you and ask that you continue to strengthen me when I feel as if I have been stripped. I pray to exalt your holy name and give you thanks for your grace and mercy. In Jesus's name, amen.

My Faith in God: I pray to be stripped of my sinful ways and renewed in my walk to serve and witness for Jesus Christ.

Confess and believe!

Today I confess giving God all the glory because he stripped me and made me over. Thank you Jesus for changing my life from the old mindset to a new way and walking in the mind of Christ.

REHABILITATED TO LIVE

If we have been united together in the likeness of His death, certainly we also shall be in the likeness of His resurrection, knowing this, that our old man was crucified with Him, that the body of sin might be done away with, that we should no longer be slaves of sin. For he who has died has been freed from sin. Now if we died with Christ, we believe that we shall also live with Him, knowing that Christ, having been raised from the dead, dies no more. Death no longer has dominion over Him. For the death that He died, He died to sin once for all; but the life that He lives, He lives to God. Likewise you also, reckon yourselves to be dead indeed to sin, but alive to God in Christ Jesus our Lord.

Therefore do not let sin reign in your mortal body, that you should obey it in its lusts. And do not present your members as instruments of unrighteousness to sin, but present yourselves to God as being alive from the dead, and your members as instruments of righteousness to God. For sin shall not have dominion over you, for you are not under law but under grace. (Romans 6:5-14)

Lord, thank you for allowing me to receive rehabilitation through the care you provide. I ask you, Lord, to stay with me as I recover from my injuries. Help me have a sound mind through my injuries. Help me keep my mind on you for all my injuries. Help me concentrate on you as my comforter and my strength while I recover. Lord, regardless of the injury, keep my heart, my soul, and my mind in your perfect will. Lord, even if I get sad for any reason, touch me with your gentle loving kindness and tender mercies. All praise to your holy name.

My Faith in God: My faith helps me seek God to be rehabilitated in the areas of life I need help in.

Confess and believe!

Today I confess giving God all the glory, for He has changed me from a jealous person to a better person. You reminded me that you can provide all of my needs.

PLAY ON MY EMOTIONS

And fear not them which kill the body, but are not able to kill the soul: but rather fear him which is able to destroy both soul and body in hell. Matthew 10:28(KJV)

You created emotions within me, and you allowed them to react according to your will and purpose for my life. At the same time, you know how to control my emotions. You know how to control my mind and my actions. You are the God who can settle me in all ways. You even said that your ways are not like ours.

Lord, please keep my emotions in check. Help me walk more in the Spirit than in emotions. Help me overcome those emotional stages of life that dampen my spiritual life. Keep my mind on you. Protect me from drugs and things that could entice me. Do not let me give in to my emotions. Lord, please do not allow the enemy to play on my emotions. Lord, send your Holy Spirit to guide my life. In Jesus's name, amen.

My Faith in God: My faith helps me to avoid sexual immorality as its states in Chapter one of the book of Romans.

Confess and believe!

Today I confess giving God all the glory because you help me to get through those emotional times when I needed you and when the enemy tried to prey on me.

ENDURE

For God is not unjust to forget your work and labor of love which you have shown toward His name, in that you have ministered to the saints, and do minister. And we desire that each one of you show the same diligence to the full assurance of hope until the end, that you do not become sluggish, but imitate those who through faith and patience inherit the promises.

For when God made a promise to Abraham, because He could swear by no one greater, He swore by Himself, saying, "Surely blessing I will bless you, and multiplying I will multiply you." And so, after he had patiently endured, he obtained the promise. (Hebrews 6:10-15)

Lord, help me endure this time in combat. Keep me in your perfect way. There is no one like you in all creation, in heaven and earth. I will look to the hills where my help comes from. Then I know that I will endure the tough times. You have the power to help me endure in my daily works and walk. You alone can give me wisdom to make good decisions. You are omnipotent and all-merciful. You bless me so much when I do not deserve any good thing. I will praise you forever, my Savior, my Lord, and my strength. In Jesus's name, amen.

My Faith in God: My faith helps me seek God to fill my thirst when I feel empty, lonely, confused, or lost. I desire that you fill me with your love, Lord Jesus Christ.

Confess and believe!

Today I confess giving God all the glory because my endurance comes from the Lord giving me strength. He is glorious and all powerful.

HEALING

And the prayer of faith will save the sick, and the Lord will raise him up, And if he has committed sins, he will be forgiven. (James 5:15)

Lord, You are the God who transcends our physicians' healing. You know how to heal when I do not see it coming. You know how to heal when doubts try to take over my belief in you.

Lord, I thank you that life can start over from surgery and operations. I thank you that life can start over after recovering from drug addiction. I thank you that life can start over with just one touch of your amazing grace. I thank you that you allowed me to see you in action in my life.

Father you are the healer and deliverer because you are the only true and all-wise God. All praise, glory, and honor and blessing to your righteous name.

My Faith in God: My faith helps me to overcome demon that prey against me using alcoholism and drug addictions.

Confess and believe!

Today I confess giving God all the glory because every time the enemy preys on me, God removes that demonic attack.

POSTPARTUM DEPRESSION

And the peace of God, which surpasses all understanding, will guard your hearts and minds through Christ Jesus. (Philippians 4:7)

Almighty God, be with me through my troubles in sickness of postpartum depression. Help me overcome it by your blessed grace. Help me speak to denounce it today by the power of your Holy Spirit. Heal me as you healed the five lepers. I thank you in advance because I know you are well able to heal no matter whatever the situation involves.

Touch me and renew my mind that it may be Christlike. You said, "Think on whatsoever things are true, whatsoever is noble, whatsoever things are just, whatsoever things are pure, whatsoever things are of good report, if there be any virtue and if there is anything praiseworthy, meditate on these things." Lord, never allow me to think in a diseased mind-set of depression.

My Faith in God: My faith helps me seek God to fill my thirst when I feel empty, lonely, confused, or lost. I desire that you fill me with your love, Lord Jesus Christ.

Confess and believe!

Today I confess that you deliver people from all kinds of issues. You deliver your people from demons of depression that prey to take lives. However, Jesus makes me more than a conqueror.

DEPRESSION

Come to Me, all you who labor and are heavy laden, and I will give you rest. Take My yoke upon you and learn from Me, for I am gentle and lowly in heart, and you will find rest for your souls. For My yoke is easy and My burden is light. (Matthew 11:28-30)

Father, I thank you for not allowing any form of depression to conquer me. Instead, by your power, I am able to regain my righteous mind in Christ Jesus.

Thank you for pulling down the stronghold of depression. I will continue to pray and exalt your name daily when the enemy attacks. Today, I have decided to give all the pressures of any anxiety or any depression attacks to you. Thank you for keeping my mind free of troubles, pain, and disease. I walk in freedom right now. Lord I ask that you keep the mind you placed in my head in a condition to glorify you. Keep the mind games and any mind setbacks away. Keep my mind on you that I will never be exposed to the enemy's plot of depression.

You said, "Let this mind be you which was also in Christ Jesus." You spoke of humility. Lord, if my mind is on you, evil is defeated. Lord, if my mind is experiencing the peace that surpasses all understanding because of your touch, the enemy is defeated again on that front. I count it all joy because you have taken my burdens away.

My Faith in God: My faith helps me seek God to fill my thirst when I feel empty, lonely, confused, or lost. I desire that you fill me with your love, Lord Jesus Christ.

Confess and believe!

Today I confess giving God all the glory, for He is the only true and wise God. Holy, holy, holy is the name of Jesus Christ. We must recognize His awesome goodness.

PERSUASION OF LOVE

Who shall separate us from the love of Christ? Shall tribulation, or distress, or persecution, or famine, or nakedness, or peril, or sword? (Romans 8:35)

Heavenly Father, you said in your word that "neither death nor life, nor angels nor principalities nor power, nor things present nor things to come, nor height nor depth, nor any other created thing shall be able to separate me from the love of God." Father, help me look to you for the ultimate love, passion, and persuasion of love.

I have been persuaded of children. I have been persuaded of marriage. They both have the impact of your love, Lord. Your love clearly helps me be relieved of doubting your love. Your love helps me overcome emptiness in my life. Your love makes the tears of my heart cry with praise in my heart, mind, and soul.

Your love is endless, because, as your word says, "God is love." You are love forever. Love is your will in our lives. Love is the key to pleasing you and keeping our lives. I will praise your name eternally.

> **My Faith in God: My faith helps me to overcome demons of sexual perversion, pride and prostitution. It is the love of Christ that keeps me when troubled times hit my life.**

Confess and believe!

Today I confess that I will ask God to fight my battles against all prey that seeks to destroy me or devour me. I believe in the power of God.

ABOUT THE AUTHOR

Joseph Harris is currently a resident of Texas. He is retired from the United States armed forces. He is the pastor and founder of Christian Worship Outreach Center Ministries. His mission is based on Matthew 16, Matthew 28, and Romans 10:9-10. Nevertheless, his focus and foundation is the word of God as the Holy Spirit guides him and this ministry. His goal is to help others receive Jesus Christ as Lord and Redeemer in their lives. His prayer is that everyone come to Jesus and become His servant with a transformed mind and heart pleasing to God. He prays that every family comes to the saving knowledge of our Lord and be equally yoked in the spirit. May God be the center force of your life and homes (Philippians 2:5; Colossians 1:18-20; Ephesians 2:8; Ephesians 6). Stand on the word of God, for His love is eternal, never ending in your life.